June 2017

To:
David a

D1553612

PITTSBURGH
DRINKS

*So you can be
well informed
bargene in Pittsburgh*

Cody and Sean make us look cool. Their speakeasy history of Pittsburgh is not only an edgy page-turner but would make for a great movie (in a city that's the backdrop for so many movies today). I can't wait to make these cocktails at my next party—and show off all of my hometown trivia (Rude Judies, all around). Adam Milliron's photography makes the drinks go down that much easier.
—Victoria Bradley-Morris, executive editor/managing director, TABLE *magazine*

Pittsburgh, my native city, is (probably not coincidentally) one of America's great drinking towns. With this fine, engaging book, it has received a deep, detailed and necessary history of just how it has been so—and continues to be so.
—Dave Wondrich, author of Imbibe!: From Absinthe Cocktail to Whiskey Smash, a Salute in Stories and Drinks to "Professor" Jerry Thomas, Pioneer of the American Bar and Punch: The Delights (and Dangers) of the Flowing Bowl

Wow. This is an eye-opener. And a taste-teaser. This gloriously researched and surprising history teaches us about our town through the speakeasies, jazz clubs, hippie haunts, discos, recent restaurants and the innovative concoctions of some of the best bartenders anywhere!
—Rick Sebak, WQED

Pittsburgh has reinvented itself in recent years, still proud of its heritage as the Steel City, now driven not by smoke and soot but by technology, medicine, art, culture, cuisine, outdoor pursuits, dining. And the evolution has been a spirited one, proven here with a lively, entertaining and informative look at how the last century or so has led to the present state of adult beverages in the Golden Triangle—a vibrant, sparkling community balancing tradition and innovation, with room at the bar for one and all, whether raising a classic cocktail, new invention or Imp 'n' Iron. Slainte!
—Lissa Brennan, City Paper

If you want to make a "Fussfungle" cocktail, Cody McDevitt and Sean Enright have written the book for you. Pittsburgh Drinks *provides a fast-paced history of the region's bars, taverns and clubs. If all that reading makes you thirsty, they augment their story with a collection of famous and forgotten drink recipes, all with links to Pittsburgh.*
—Len Barcousky, author of Hidden History of Pittsburgh

PITTSBURGH
DRINKS

A History of
Cocktails, Nightlife & Bartending Tradition

Cody McDevitt and Sean Enright

AMERICAN PALATE

Published by American Palate
A Division of The History Press
Charleston, SC
www.historypress.net

Copyright © 2017 by Cody McDevitt and Sean Enright
All rights reserved

Front cover: Photo by Adam Milliron.

Back cover, bottom: Jazz band, with Jimmy Smith on organ, possibly Eddie
McFadden on guitar and possibly Donald Bailey on drums, performing in
Hurricane Club. *Charles Teenie Harris, American, 1908–1998, 1953–56, Pittsburgh;
photograph © 2016 Carnegie Museum of Art, Pittsburgh, Charles "Teenie" Harris Archive*;
inset: Photo by Adam Milliron.

First published 2017

Manufactured in the United States

ISBN 9781467137782

Library of Congress Control Number: 2016956928

For all those who came before and those who will come after.

CONTENTS

FOREWORD

I've long been fond of telling folks as they experience a cocktail for the first time, "Ignorance isn't bliss. It's a vodka tonic."

When I came of drinking age in Pittsburgh in 1995, I drank a lot of vodka tonics, a lot of Yuengling and a lot of very bad shots of whiskey and tequila. The one indignity I am proud to say I remained ignorant of was a passion for light beer. I'm proud to live in bliss where that is concerned.

Before I left Pittsburgh in 2002, my favorite places to drink were Dee's Café and the Lava Lounge in the South Side. I had for the most part not the slightest notion of what a well-made cocktail was. I'm pretty sure I didn't know they existed. I clearly remember, however, my very first experience with a well-made drink. It was at the Tiki Lounge, with Don Bistarkey behind the bar on a slower night. Before I could order anything, he made me a drink he'd recently discovered and had been fiddling around with. It was called a "mojito," and it was the tastiest damn alcoholic beverage I had ever tasted. I went back to drinking my highballs and beer soon after, but that initial drink stuck with me. Don was also responsible for my first taste of rye whiskey. Kevin Brown and I asked for shots of Jack Daniels as usual, but Don, consistent booze educator that he was, pulled out a bottle of Heaven Hill Rye and poured that instead. It didn't go down well, and I thought I'd never drink it again.

But Don had planted a seed.

I'd been working in restaurants and bars in Pittsburgh since I was about twenty-one. So when I wound up in New York, I looked for jobs in hospitality. I had oodles of experience waiting tables but was looking for a new challenge. I wanted to work in a bar. I had had two underwhelming bartending jobs in Pittsburgh and knew that experience wasn't going to cut the mustard in the New York City market. I decided to find a barback position.

I responded to an open call at the Flatiron Lounge about six weeks after it had opened. The "cocktail resurgence" was just beginning. At this time, the only two recognized cocktail bars in NYC were Milk and Honey and Angel Share.

I got the job.

I clearly remember my first night working there. I watched in awe as Julie Reiner crafted cocktails with four, then five, then six or more ingredients.

I thought to myself, "What the hell is going on here?"

At the end of my shift, the staff was allowed to choose a cocktail to familiarize us with the menu. I picked the Metropolis. It was vodka infused with Granny Smith apples and a bit of apple brandy. I was astounded by how good it was. I had no idea it was only the tip of an emerging iceberg. I had no idea how fortunate I was to have stumbled into what was going to be one of the first bars to bring back quality cocktails to the masses. It would change New York City nightlife's drinking scene, my life and eventually the palates of people living as far away as my hometown, Pittsburgh, Pennsylvania.

I stayed at Flatiron Lounge for three years, eventually becoming the head bartender. I moved along and grew with the expanding cocktail scene in New York City. I was head bartender at Pegu Club and then bar manager at Death + Co., and I eventually opened my own bar, Mayahuel, in 2009.

I did consulting as the cocktail culture grew into other markets across the country, such as San Diego, and as far away as Hong Kong and Australia. In 2011, I got a phone call from Steve Zumoff about a new bar called the Rowdy Buck that he and Scott Kramer, owners of Lava Lounge and Tiki Lounge, were opening back in Pittsburgh. They wondered if I would like to help them with a cocktail list. I'd kept in touch with Scott and Steve over the years, and we'd often discuss the trends in the New York City cocktail culture and how they could adapt those trends to a cocktail bar in the Pittsburgh market. I knew the Rowdy Buck was not the ideal place to do cocktails in Pittsburgh's rediscovered cocktail market. It was right in the middle of the notorious shit storm–party avenue that is East Carson Street on the South Side. It was too large a venue to provide a consistent, well-crafted cocktail to the masses who invaded the South Side on the weekends, but I was game to give it a shot.

Well, the cocktail scene at the Rowdy Buck never took off, but it was still a good experience. The bartenders were all eager and curious and dedicated to the idea of making cocktails instead of "bombs" of all varieties and the normal run-of-the-mill libations indigenous to East Carson Street. However, the space was too big, and the business eventually had to bow to the demands of its customer base, who flooded the new establishment as surely as they flooded the other watering holes that lined Carson Street.

The friends and family of the Rowdy Buck were an entirely different animal. It was early in the week, and people were coming for the cocktails. It was like working in a cocktail bar in Pittsburgh! A fair number of the patrons were bartenders from other bars from around the city. The cocktail renaissance was taking hold in Pittsburgh, and I began to meet the movers and shakers of that movement. I was unaware how far along the Pittsburgh scene had come, as I rarely made it home. And when I did, I generally sought out the nostalgia of my old haunts. We talked about what bars they worked at and what kind of drinks were popular with people. It was inspiring to hear that there really was a cocktail culture growing in Da 'Burgh.

It was on one of those nights I had a very curious experience that I must admit I was really proud of. A bartender from a downtown hotel bar asked me for a "Final Ward." A Final Ward is a variation on the Last Word I had created at the Pegu Club roughly seven years earlier. This guy had no idea who I was or that I had invented it. I asked him where he had heard of the Final Ward, and he said, "I believe it's a classic?" The Final Ward is arguably the second most replicated of my original cocktails, so it wasn't completely outlandish that this guy in Pittsburgh had read of it and even served it in his bar. However, it gave the growing drinking culture of the city a good dose of legitimacy in my mind. It opened my eyes to how far the professionals had brought the new cocktail culture to Pittsburgh. There were bartenders all over the city researching drinks, studying history and adapting recipes of other bartenders from other cities. I always stress that paramount to becoming a good bartender is taking what you can from bartenders the world over and then understanding their processes to help evolve those ideas for the future generations.

It's incredible how quickly things can change. As Don Bistarkey taught me, you just need to plant the seed, and a cocktail culture will flourish. Who would have thought five years ago there would be a Pittsburgh cocktail book? I was very proud—and remain so to this day—of my contribution to the reinvention of the cocktail in New York City over the past decade. I'm sure it is akin to what the bartenders in Pittsburgh, who made this book possible, must likewise feel. Congrats. And Amen.

—Phil Ward
Mayahuel
New York City, 2016

ACKNOWLEDGEMENTS

I want to thank my family for their love and support throughout the years. My sisters, Hilary and Kelly, are my best friends, along with my brother, Casey, and brother-in-law, AJ. My nephew, Jackson, is the joy of my life. My dad has been an inspiration to me—and it was the memory of him writing legal briefs from morning until night on his days off that gave me the work ethic and drive needed to write a book like this. My mom has always encouraged me to pursue my dreams, and she has been my biggest fan throughout hard times and good. And my stepmom, Lori, the Saks Fifth Avenue girl, has always been the hip figure in my life who knew what the nightlife is and was like. She was and is much cooler than I'll ever be, and her insights were invaluable. I'd like to thank my friends Steve Yudelson, George Janusz, Mikey Pacella and Jeremy Norman for listening to me talk about the book for hours on end. Eric Boyd and George Fattman were insightful and improved the book tremendously with their edits. I'd also like to thank Karmen Cook for giving two unpublished writers the chance to show their work to the world by offering us a book deal. Linda Parker, of the *Pittsburgh Post-Gazette*, was indispensable in our search for old photos. I'd like to thank my two collaborators on the project, Sean Enright and Adam Milliron. And I deeply appreciate all the bartenders and the chef who contributed recipes. And finally I want to thank my newspaper editor, Brian Whipkey, and all the staff and employees at the *Somerset Daily American* for their support and friendship. Writing can be a tough life, but moments and compositions like this make the endless hours of coffee, typing and microfilm worth it.

—Cody McDevitt

ACKNOWLEDGEMENTS

First and foremost, I would thank my children, Colwyn and Alexis, who have been the greatest achievements of my life. Their love inspires me every day. Special thanks to my mother, Judith Enright, and brother, Patrick Enright, who have always been my greatest supporters. I'm fortunate to have close relationships with my cousins, aunts, uncles and other family members in the Enright, Erion, Cavanaugh, O'Brien and Murphy clan. The Pittsburgh dining community has made this book possible. Thank you to the Café Allegro, Big Burrito, Spoon/BRGR, Lava/Tiki Lounge and Bar Marco families for helping me grow in my profession. It has been an extreme honor to represent the Pittsburgh bartending community. Thank you bartenders and Pittsburgh's chapter of the United States Bartenders' Guild for your continuous passion, knowledge, hospitality and inspiration. Most notably, Bethany Tryc, Summer Voelker, Maggie Meskey, Fred Sarkis, Don Bistarkey, Lexi Rebert, D.C. Huntley and Heather Enright have all inspired and supported my passion for the craft in different ways. Thank you to all the contributors to this project, without whose submissions we would not have as complete a picture of Pittsburgh's cocktail scene as we now do. And finally, thanks to my writing partner, Cody. Together we are proud to present this unique tribute to Pittsburgh cocktails. Slàinte mhaith! Tip your bartenders!

—SEAN DWYER ENRIGHT

Unless otherwise noted, recipes and instructions are given by Sean Enright.

INTRODUCTION

Pittsburgh drinkers, dancers, deejays and drink-makers have brought and taken with them various fashions and tastes throughout the city's existence. Periodically in the city's history, the popular places and people have passed away, forgotten with the arrival of the new and trendy. But during all those transitions, the city maintained a central identity, one that served as the basis for the new places locals visited when they left the mills, mines, hospitals or other workplaces after their job was finished for the day.

The larger course of Pittsburgh's nightlife traces the time of widowed and uneducated bartenders on the South Side to the current period of sophisticated gastropubs filled with mixologists who earned degrees at prestigious four-year universities. It has taken drinkers through speakeasies, cafés, lounges and jazz clubs. It has seen them dancing in discos and nightclubs. It takes them into Smoking Joe's to argue over sports with working-class bartenders. It leads them into Jimmy D's for shots while they're watching people dance.

The drinking history of the city is inextricably bound to its larger history as a great American city. Local historians often focus on the Carnegie, the Mellon and the Heinz families or key in on mayors and politicians as the important figures shaping Pittsburgh's destiny. They often forget that most movements start with conversations, and a great deal of those conversations began while people had their elbow bent at the bar, drinking some concoction composed by a well-informed bartender who had their ear to the ground.

Pittsburgh is not only forging a new cocktail culture. It is beginning to rediscover its old one. It's our history, and we should never dismiss it as being lesser than those of New York, Chicago, Los Angeles or New Orleans. It may not win national awards, but it's something to be proud of.

The bar and spirit history of Pittsburgh is its people's history. It's the story of its heroes, villains, lovers and sages mingling to create the perception of the city held by visitors and locals alike. It's who we are and what we've been.

—CODY MCDEVITT

PART I

WHAT WE'VE BEEN

1

SPEAKEASIES UP TO PROHIBITION

In 1901, a newspaper editor sent a reporter to a speakeasy on Pittsburgh's South Side to see whether it had police protection and to write about such establishments as one of the city's evils.

When the reporter arrived at the scene, he saw a police officer standing a block away from the establishment, watching men and women walk in freely.

The speakeasy had no password, no need to verify if someone was the law or not. People came and went without speaking to an employee through a slot opening. It contradicted the perception of speakeasies as being secretive and subversive.

In the speakeasy, the reporter saw a well-furnished and nice interior, with the only eyesore being the two black eyes of the female bartender, which had been left on her by a previous patron.

The speakeasy culture had started a little more than a decade before in the city and had started in western Pennsylvania long before it became a well-known term during Prohibition.

Speakeasies arose after the passage of the Brook's High License Law, which was enacted in 1888. The legislation raised the cost of a saloon license to $500—a hefty price that most people couldn't afford to pay if they wanted to sell alcohol.

Speakeasy was a term coined in Pittsburgh by Kate Hester of McKeesport. She defied the law, and many of her customers were a boisterous lot, according to a *New York Times* account.

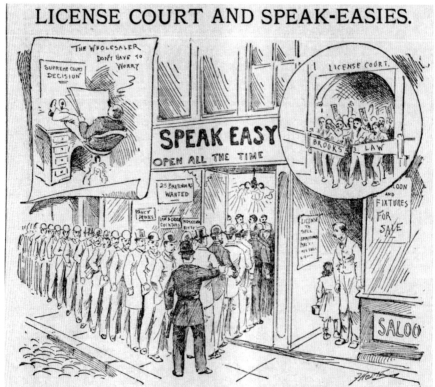

What We May See if the Policy of No License and No Police Interference is Continued for Another Year.

When the Brook's High License Law was passed, saloon licenses became much more expensive. Speakeasies were more economically feasible. *Photo courtesy of the* Pittsburgh Post-Gazette.

When they got too rowdy, she would approach them with a raised finger and an awe-inspiring look while telling them to "Speak easy, boys! Speak easy."

The expression became common and spread to Pittsburgh, where the newspaper reporters used it in reference to all illicit establishments run by people unwilling to pay the license fee.

"Some day, perhaps, Webster's Dictionary will take it up," the *Times* said about the word in the 1890s.

Even if saloonkeepers had the money, the licenses were hard to come by. Licenses were not granted on charity. People who received them had to be seen as strong and important members of society—that and a few connections would help.

Hester, of McKeesport, applied for a license, but her application was defective. She was given a hearing where she produced a letter from her pastor giving her a good name.

In sheriffs' sales, saloons that went out of business would be sold along with their licenses.

"There is considerable hue and cry over the large number of sheriff's sales of saloons," a courthouse official told the *Pittsburgh Daily Post* early in the speakeasy era. "The great trouble with the saloonkeeper is debt. Many of them go into the business with a big debt hanging over them."

ONE OF McTIGHE'S POLICEMEN GETTING A DRINK IN THE BIG DIAMOND STREET SPEAKEASY.

Policemen would often infiltrate the speakeasy culture undercover to gather information on proprietors. *Photo courtesy of the* Pittsburgh Post-Gazette.

Saloonkeepers would face liens of up to $10,000 once they secured a liquor license. The brewers or wholesale liquor dealers who supplied them alcohol held the liens.

"I tell you the saloon business is getting worse everyday [*sic*] instead of better," George Mashey, a well-known downtown saloonkeeper, said. "The fellows that are sold out by the sheriff are the victims of poor business, and that is all there is to it. The great obstacles the licensed saloonkeeper must contend with today are the clubroom and the speakeasy. They are flourishing, it seems better now than they ever did."

Because saloons were cost prohibitive and difficult to get a license for, speakeasies became the predominant establishments where people drank.

Speakeasies changed the drinking habits in Pittsburgh. Saloons were not places of public drunkenness. And they closed at a certain time. So there was a limit to how intoxicated a man could get while in a bar. One government agent said in 1890:

> *Speakeasies are the cause of a great deal more drunkenness than legitimate saloons. When a man goes into a resort of this kind, he will usually remain there long enough to imbibe a half dozen glasses of liquor, and stay until he gets drunk.*
>
> *The patrons of these places are mostly mill men and employees in factories who have been in the habit of going to a saloon, taking a drink and walking out. Now they will be found loafing in these places.*

In Pittsburgh's early nightlife, bartenders, saloonkeepers and speakeasy proprietors showed a penchant for creativity.

Cocktails were popular throughout the pre-Prohibition speakeasy era. Most cocktail historians peg the time falling between 1860 and 1930 as the golden era of cocktails. Pittsburgh was no different from other major metropolitan areas in following trends set elsewhere.

The newspapers of the time carried accounts of what drinks were popular in cities like Chicago and New York City. Their ingredients often accompanied the cocktails' names. Bartenders in the city would read the accounts and make them for their customers.

In a number of advertisements for produce and groceries in the late nineteenth century, the innovation undertaken by local barkeeps was mentioned.

They would market fresh ingredients, such as pineapples and strawberries and other things, to muddle into their drinks. The use of turnips by bartenders appeared in one account.

HOW THEY DRANK YESTERDAY AT "MUSTY" PRICE'S PLACE.

Though speakeasies were often held in disrepute, a wide swath of the public drank in them, including people who dressed in top hats and three-piece suits. *Photo courtesy of the* Pittsburgh Post-Gazette.

As early as 1870, fancy drinks were revealed as popular features at local saloons. A drink called a "Red Planet," with unknown ingredients, was singled out in the newspaper as one of the most popular beverages in the city.

In a 1902 *Brooklyn Daily Eagle* article, the reporter said a new drink had been introduced to New York City from Pittsburgh. It was called the "Fussfungle" and had been created in McKeesport.

The cocktail included pure spirits, water, burned brown sugar and molasses. The Slavic people invented it, and it was highly alcoholic. It was said to cause fights in church. The *Daily Eagle* said:

Interior View of the Third Avenue Speakeasy Presided Over by Claudia Welsh, Where No Fear of Any Police Interference Is Felt.

A rendering of Claudia Welsh's Speakeasy that appeared in the *Pittsburgh Weekly Gazette* in a December 1902. *Photo courtesy of the* Pittsburgh Post-Gazette.

With a few pints of this delectable compound circulating through his system the merrymaker takes joy in shooting holes through the persons of his family and choicest friends.

He is ready to carry an election with it, or to dance down the strongest set of legs in his social circle, or to get up a strike, or to burn his house, or to do almost anything else that will express his high vitality and joy. The only trouble about it is that the police will not always let him.

The mayor of McKeesport tried to persuade his parishioners to avoid the drink and imbibe gin. Nevertheless, the Fussfungle became a nationally popular drink and was compared in popularity to absinthe, the prevailing drink in France.

Another drink that became popular locally was the Braddock Highball. It was built on the lines of an ordinary highball, but it had a splatter of vinegar, a sprinkle of pepper, a pinch of salt and a dash of ginger.

"The Braddock highball is more entangling than the McKeesport Fussfungle, and the man who sticks to it will probably feel as rich as a billionaire, but will feel correspondingly poor when he gets sober," said the Green Goods Man, a special commentator who frequently described cocktails in the *Pittsburgh Daily Post* during the turn of the century.

Though there was strong opposition from dry forces against drunkenness, there were also citizens who thought speakeasies served an important function in the city.

David Lauber, who owned Newell's Old Stand on Fifth Avenue, told a newspaper in 1890 that he thought speakeasies unburdened saloons from having too many customers.

Interior of Yee Hing's Speakeasy on Robinson Street as it was in 1901. *Photo courtesy of the Pittsburgh Post-Gazette.*

"This city is a great place for drinking. So far as I am personally concerned, I do not object to speakeasies, because they take a certain trade that I don't want," Lauber said. "The relief from the surplus of speak-easies will be found in more saloons well distributed."

A Smithfield Street saloonkeeper even told the newspaper that he would gladly see half of his customers go somewhere else to get their drinks because it was impossible to attend to their wants properly.

He said he would rather sell less and have more room. He had four bartenders in a place that was fit for three.

The west end of the city did not contain any licensed saloons, but it had more speakeasies than any other neighborhood.

A judge told a reporter that the reason he refused a license to residents in that part of town was he did not think anyone in the area was competent enough to conduct a saloon.

The South Side became a very profitable place for speakeasy owners. There were four mills there, three glass houses and manufacturers of other sorts. When the saloons closed, the employees started visiting the speakeasies.

Speakeasies were open on Sunday, which often offended the religious temperance leaders, who were amassing power in the years before Prohibition.

Some of the speakeasies were places of squalor. On Spruce Alley, between Thirtieth and Thirty-First Streets, officers puked when entering the area because it smelled so bad. It was operated by Mrs. Bessie Shea, a widow.

The alley near it was swarming with men, women and children, all mixed together in mud up to their ankles. There were a thousand people there, according to the *Daily Post*. Dissipated men were cursing half-clad children as they picked their way through the mud puddles. All ages and genders were drinking at the party. Mostly women operated the row of houses. Most of the boys in the South Side went to Lower St. Clair Township to party. People couldn't go a few blocks without seeing a crime committed. Young women were brought there and gotten drunk.

Father Fisher, a pastor, had heard of the depravity in Lower St. Clair Township. "Why there is one man who is said to be, on good authority, at the same time both father and grandfather to a 17-year-old," Fisher said. "The place certainly needs to be morally purged, but I do not like to see it done in any unlawful and violent manner. The whipping post would be a good thing for some of these people, however."

When a man brutally beat his wife, a group of men showed up at his house to teach him a lesson. The man was severely flogged.

Kegs and beer stands were kept in yards instead of hen houses. People were often shot upon entering an establishment.

There would be fights and murders, rabble and ruffians outside many speakeasies. The city's reputation for toughness started in the speakeasy era, which began only a few decades after the Industrial Revolution.

In the late nineteenth century there was a running riot on the South Side every Sunday.

Neighbors complained of destructive beer picnics. Several young men in that district had leased a grove in the suburbs and held picnics there every Sunday. Beer and whiskey were liberally supplied for cash.

The credit system was unknown. The men and women who attended those picnics indulged freely, and as a result, the events usually ended in a midnight brawl.

Speakeasies also floated throughout Pittsburgh. A speakeasy boathouse was located on the Allegheny River. A tough crowd that lived nearby in camps frequented it. At these camps, the ostensible occupation was fishing.

Some illegal practices were there. Days in camp were spent loafing, relieved occasionally by snake-hunting, frog-chasing or similar sports. Evenings were spent listening to music from instruments such as accordions, banjos and so forth, as well as drinking, singing, shouting and spinning yarns. Liquor was, as the newspaper put it, the spirit of camp life, and the boathouse was one of the leading venues.

Camp life on the Allegheny bank beyond Aspinwall had some of the delights of utopia, but the camp was filled with vice. Many ex-convicts were among the half-frantic crew of the boathouse, according to the *Pittsburgh Daily Post*.

Within the speakeasy culture, there was a form of liquor sales called walking speakeasies, a phrase coined for people who strolled through the streets offering drinks to strangers walking near them. One walking speakeasy during the early era was a stylish-looking mulatto named William Coles, who carried a bottle of whiskey and a revolver into the mining communities and sold liquor. The gun was needed to discourage the rough workers from stealing his supply.

Some speakeasy proprietors would send little girls to stop men in the street who looked thirsty. The girl would ask them if they wanted a drink. If the answer were yes, the girl would go into the speakeasy and return with a bottle of whiskey, receiving payment in return.

Lawbreakers and speakeasy owners were permitted to run so long as they voted for specific candidates. Police took down the names of people who visited speakeasies, tallying the number of votes they could control. Saloonkeepers and speakeasy operators were often asked by police and government officials to give money in addition to rallying support.

Though the city was known for its steelworkers who drank, there was a group of literati who also enjoyed grabbing a cocktail or two.

Exclusive speakeasies were known as clubhouses. Between three and four hundred were located throughout the city in the early speakeasy era in Pittsburgh. No member was permitted to bring any outsider into the clubs on Sunday, although they could introduce one more club member a week. The clubs usually consisted of six to twenty men who rented a room and paid a certain amount per month for a janitor, liquor and rent. At many places, they did not pay for the drinks they received; instead, the drinks were part of the membership costs. Members were ejected from the clubroom as soon as they got drunk, so they were not much trouble to the police.

In 1890, police did uncover a club on the South Side called the Black Eagle Club, located on 2907 Sarah Street. The proprietor was Michael Leofky. The clubroom was in a cellar, and a book was found therein. The title page read, "Black Eagle Club. We, the members, agree to abide by the laws of the Black Eagle club, an organization for the promotion of the social and literary propensities of its members." The pages contained numerous names of prominent South Side citizens. The Black Eagle Club had a library. The men in the club became members by paying twenty-five cents. The proprietor would be supplied with beer and liquor, and the customer's account would be kept. The privileged ones could commune in silence with their favorite authors and dodge the dripping beer that ran through the cracks in the floor overhead.

In Soho, an eighty-six-acre parcel opposite the South Side, a club found by police was very stylish in furnishings and the liquors kept there. A stock of champagne and fine wines was also kept there. Alexander P. Schaub, a professor of music and a son of a former Smithfield Street confectioner, operated it. His apartment was a three-room apartment with a kitchen speakeasy.

Visitors to the club included professional men, musicians, gilded youths and holders of public positions; among the latter were a number of young ladies who were employed in city and county offices.

In 1893, a gilded speakeasy, one of the highly exclusive kind where gentlemen only were admitted, was raided. It was a luxuriously furnished apartment operated by a Jewish man named Jim Simonton and his wife, Jane. Jane would station herself at the second-story front window when the speakeasy was in operation. From there, she could observe who was coming in. If the visitors were deemed safe to enter, she would touch an electric button by her side, which would give her husband notice that it was OK for him to open the door. The thirsty men would pass to the buffet parlor in the rear. When they were busted, the button wasn't working.

Lee Frazier, a well-known politician of Allegheny, was arrested in 1894 for selling liquor illegally on Sunday and to minors. He started a club called the Tammany Tigers in Allegheny. Mothers complained about their boys coming home drunk after visiting his club.

The front page of a 1901 *Pittsburgh Weekly Gazette* shows how prevailing the speakeasy was in Pittsburgh before Prohibition. *Photo courtesy of the* Pittsburgh Post-Gazette.

Jack Sterling and Mrs. Conley's dive in the downtown district was one of the most notorious and best known in the city in the 1890s. He was busted multiple times, but he had connections and got off with a relatively cheap fifty-dollar fine by giving the promise not to open a speakeasy again. Instead, he started giving private keys, which limited the busts.

Police officers were clever in tricking proprietors into admitting them regardless of the type of club or speakeasy. If the offenders catered to a high-class customer, then the officer wore an upscale shirt and a flashy necktie and spent the department's money without concern for expenses.

In the 1890s, Officer Nick Bendle earned the nickname "Speakeasy Nick" because he could spot a speakeasy easier than any of his fellow officers. He would whisper to them that he smelled beer, and the three other officers who accompanied him on his patrols did not dream of disputing his claim.

Some policemen exhibited extraordinary bravery when busting speakeasies. Police captain Henry G. Alt of the South Side, standing six feet two inches and weighing close to two hundred pounds, executed a raid in which he set a new mark in police annals. Single-handedly, he arrested ten people in a Carson Street raid. He went into a widow's speakeasy, where he saw nine husky Irishmen. He couldn't call the patrol wagon because they would escape.

"If one of you move, there will be about ten wakes in this neighborhood for the next three days," the captain said. The bluff worked, and nobody moved. He found a small boy to bribe. The boy called the police wagon.

In another daring raid, a religious figure took on the speakeasies alone. Reverend John G. Beane, assistant at St. Paul's Cathedral and president of the local branches of the Catholic Total Abstinence society, fell upon a speakeasy within the limits of the cathedral parish and routed the people who were congregated there. Mary Sullivan owned the speakeasy he raided. A drunk man ran into him because he wanted to use too much of the sidewalk. He and the priest got into an altercation. The man ran into a speakeasy, followed by the priest.

The muscular priest slammed the door, and it became a rough house.

"Now," said the priest. "Let me have a drink, Mrs. Sullivan, and I'll see how many I know in this place."

Sullivan didn't fill the order. People rushed out the door when he came in, trying to evade the police who soon followed. The priest went to the police department and told them what happened.

Despite official orders to cease, speakeasies and drinking clubs flourished on the South Side. The stern mandate was, to all outward appearances, implicitly obeyed. But appearances were deceiving. Speakeasies and clubs flourished with vigor. It required no watchful eye to detect the willful violation of the law.

On Seventeenth Street, a club that had been disbanded was at full blast following a campaign against the speakeasies in 1891. A *Pittsburgh Daily Post* reporter entered and saw six young men seated about a deal table playing poker. Buttons were the substitutes for chips. In one corner was a pile of empty beer bottles, and on a sloppy sideboard were a number of overturned whiskey glasses.

There were some legislative efforts to reduce the cost of a liquor license from $500 to $300. Others pushed to increase the cost of a liquor license from $500 to $1,000 in order to push for prohibition in the early speakeasy era.

Speakeasies were of chief concern to police on the North Side. The establishments seemed to flourish in both poor and rich communities.

Women ran most speakeasies in that part of town and elsewhere. Many of them were either widows with large families they needed to support, or they were sickly and unable to earn money. In a city where mortality was high due to the hard occupations prevalent, many women were left with no choice but to take up an illegal and lucrative trade in lieu of being a housewife. Sympathy for their poverty often led judges and police to be easy on them. And the women often had political backing because they were able to rally support for candidates.

Historically, men are more often credited with a large chunk of innovation in drink creation, which may be due to the sexism exhibited by the liquor historians who wrote the accounts. To say that women were not blending ingredients at Pittsburgh speakeasies and shaping the cocktails nationwide can only be believed if one discounts their imagination and creativity.

One of the most popular speakeasies on Diamond Street belonged to "Honey" O'Neil. Honey was a man, but his customers were largely women. It was described as a resort of one of the most disorderly characters. Low women, both old and young, along with petty thieves and other degraded persons, were customers. In addition to the drinking rooms at O'Neil's, there was a room set apart where pictures of nude women in indecent postures adorned the walls. They were exhibited for twenty-five cents. The revenue from the room was almost constant. Women insisted on taking their companions into the room to see the exhibitions. There were still men-only rooms at O'Neil's, but women had their own quarters to drink, and many drank themselves silly.

Women were at the center of most nightlife. Brothels often populated areas where speakeasies were located. Men would often go from what was considered one sin to commit another. Women fulfilled most of their desires.

The relationship between speakeasy owners and police was frequently cozy. Around the turn of the century, an Allegheny City bartender told the *Pittsburgh Weekly Gazette*, "We're not afraid of any crusade. We haven't been notified to close yet. Whenever there's anything doin', they'll let us know in time to close."

The general consensus for speakeasy proprietors was that you paid police for their protection. If they could rally votes for a political machine, then they could also get police protection. Blackmail was common practice. The election ring, comprising police officers, would stop charging speakeasy

The interior of Honey O'Neil's Speakeasy, a popular drinking spot for women in the early twentieth century. *Photo courtesy of the* Pittsburgh Post-Gazette.

proprietors when elections would come up. They didn't want to lose votes or money contributed by speakeasy owners.

But it was something that was not told to reporters. In 1902, Mamie Weber, a speakeasy proprietor, boasted of speakeasy protection, and the police busted her place because of it.

"I conducted my place quietly and thought I was all right," Weber said to the *Pittsburgh Weekly Gazette*. "I told my customers so. The police know where I buy my beer and I thought the beer men stood ace high. It was not my intention to boast about the protection but only to assure customers they were safe in my place."

Allegheny City, which is the area now known as the North Side, had a Wild West feel to it. There were casinos, brothels and speakeasies throughout the city. It was a middle-class neighborhood prior to the rise of speakeasies, but bars and gambling houses took over and property values dropped. Tough crowds made the neighborhoods there unfriendly. People who would report speakeasies in the neighborhood were insulted and harassed. They were told to move out.

East Robinson Street was in high demand before the rise of speakeasies in Allegheny City. Efforts to rid the community of vice were ineffective. When one speakeasy owner would move out, another moved in.

In 1901, the most fashionable speakeasy in Allegheny City was found in a large red brick house on Church Street with the words "Republican Club" painted on the door. Men gathered outside the doorway while drinking. Ex-deputy sheriff William Arbogast worked the door. He was also the proprietor. He was a welcoming presence for people coming in. Men of all ages would drink beer out of bottles and glasses at his club. A great deal of nonmembers visited the place. When the beer sold out, whiskey was always available. Arbogast would eventually seek the nomination for sheriff on the labor ticket, and his campaign coffers were flush with money he made from the speakeasy he operated.

The low-order speakeasies were found in alleys. Visitors would still find a range of people, but the rougher, working-class people were typically in these bars.

The most pretentious speakeasy visited in Pittsburgh was the "Independent Rod and Gun Club" on Third Avenue. You could get a great deal of drinks at the establishment. There were drunks who visited, but it was mostly orderly.

The place central to entertainment in downtown from 1900 to 1919 was a recreation complex near the point on the Allegheny River side. The complex featured a castle-like main building bigger than Madison Square Garden. On its grounds were a roller coaster, a merry go-round and other rides.

In the East End, there was a music hall at the Carnegie Institution that would turn the neighborhood into a popular destination for people in the city, according to a *Post-Gazette* article by Bob Hoover.

Forbes Field in Oakland also attracted people to the area for nightlife entertainment.

The only times the speakeasies and gambling houses would close was prior to an election, when the word was put down by the political bosses to close them because there was a push for a reform movement from speakeasy opponents. The hope would be to diminish the coverage in the newspapers and thus make it an irrelevant issue during the election. When campaigns ended in Pittsburgh, the machine candidates would buy drinks for the patrons and say it was on the house as a reward for their support.

By some accounts, the speakeasy trade was the best paying in Pittsburgh.

The Catholic Total Abstinence Union pushed for prohibition of the speakeasies early in the twentieth century. The organization was one of the more influential groups in Pittsburgh pushing for Prohibition. There was a backlash against the culture of alcoholism that was forming in the city. Pittsburgh was hard drinking, and speakeasies had become a given in people's lives. The Prohibition movement was gaining steam. And nationally, the Prohibition forces were gathering support with reform movements pushing for a national amendment banning the manufacturing and sale of alcohol.

Women were largely behind the Prohibition push nationally. Pittsburgh had a Woman's Christian Temperance Union, but along with it, there was a large group of female speakeasy proprietors that was among the most powerful groups in the city.

The Prohibition fight in Pittsburgh often focused on legal distributors rather than the prevailing speakeasies. The Anti-Saloon League was criticized for going after only licensed saloon dealers. The criticism was fair since most of the drinking problem was found in establishments that were operating illegally.

There began to be a push to rid the city of alcohol in 1912. One of the approaches the city took was to control and regulate manufacturing rather than the sales of alcohol. This would eventually become the basis for Prohibition when it began later in the decade.

One of the organizations that pushed for the elimination of speakeasies was the Allegheny County Liquor Dealers' Protective Association. It made a list of two thousand speakeasies to target. The dealers argued that speakeasies had caused the legitimate trade to lose more than 40 percent damage annually. They argued that retail dealers couldn't pay their rents or make profits as a result.

They eventually put together a corps of detectives for the association to gather evidence against speakeasies and clubs. District attorney William A. Blakely declared open war against the illegal traffic of liquor in Allegheny County after the association submitted the evidence. The officers were threatened with prison time if they didn't make a vigilant effort to rid the city of speakeasies.

In the years approaching Prohibition, politicians began taking a hard stance against speakeasies and campaigning on pledges to rid the city of alcohol. Prohibition would become the law of the land in 1920 with the passage of the Eighteenth Amendment, which banned the sale, manufacturing and distribution of alcohol.

It remained to be seen if an official prohibition of alcohol would curtail drinking in Pittsburgh. Speakeasies had been a part of life for three decades before the ban was enacted, regardless of whether they were violating

WORKING A SPEAK-EASY.

First Copper—Come down with your voluntary campaign contribution.
Second Copper—We've never troubled you before.
Third Copper—And we never will again——
Chorus of Coppers—As long as you pay for your privileges.

Women dominated the speakeasy racket in Pittsburgh prior to Prohibition. And the police demanded payment for their protection. *Photo courtesy of the* Pittsburgh Post-Gazette.

the law; they weren't going anywhere. The new challenge for speakeasy proprietors was finding product to sell to customers.

So the ease with which liquor could be obtained suddenly went away, as did the quality of alcohol. There would need to be a new source of beer and a new provider of the whiskey that permitted steelworkers to unwind after a tough day at the mill.

While the sellers before Prohibition were concerned with the law and losing bottling licenses, the ones who would take their place in the 1920s were often brutal criminals who were indifferent to murder and other horrible acts. The Prohibition-era figures were at once beloved and feared. But they changed the drinking culture in the city forever.

Fussfungle: Pittsburgh's Pre-Prohibition Drink of Choice

The original recipe was developed in McKeesport, just outside Pittsburgh. It became popular in New York City and nationwide in the early part of the twentieth century.

1 ounce burnt brown sugar–molasses syrup (recipe follows)
2 ounces Rittenhouse Bottle In Bond 100-Proof Rye Whiskey

Add ingredients to a mixing glass, starting with less expensive syrup. After the components are included, add your ice. Hold your bar spoon as a pencil, insert into the glass, spoon side down, and rotate clockwise along the edge of the glass, holding the spoon loosely so it can turn with the edge of the glass. The cup of the spoon should always be facing the center as you stir. A perfect stir should be noiseless. This takes time to master. The key is to allow the spoon to swivel and spin between your fingers as you move your hand. You need a relaxed grasp on the spoon to allow it to turn with the current of your stir. Once your cocktail is chilled, strain over a large ice cube in a rocks glass.

Burnt Brown Sugar–Molasses Syrup
½ cup brown sugar
½ cup water
¼ cup molasses

Heat brown sugar in a small saucepan until sugar begins to darken on the edges. Stir and continue to cook over medium heat until melted and darkened further. Remove from heat and add water. Stir until sugar has dissolved fully. Then add molasses. Stir until molasses has dissolved. Remove from heat and refrigerate for up to one month.

2

PROHIBITION IN PITTSBURGH

J.W. "Kid" Miller was a legend in the Hill District. Before Prohibition began in 1920, Miller kept bar at the Sutton Emporium in lower Wylie.

"In his day the dapper 'Kid' was as nifty a bartender as ever fooled a cash register," a writer for the *Pittsburgh Daily Courier* said in a 1925 article.

But Prohibition forced Kid to break ground and move from spot to spot in the Hill District. He would not surrender his craft without a fight. He retreated to "Shady" Avenue before moving farther out on Wylie again.

"It certainly seems a shame to see an artist who used to shake the mixed drinks in the air be forced to ease one's potion to a customer in a tea cup and a whisper," the *Courier* said. "The art of the calling is lost."

But the writer was mistaken.

Throughout the city, speakeasies, clubs and cabarets popped up to satisfy the city's need for nightlife. Bartenders continued to innovate cocktails, particularly in the Hill District, where jazz influenced bartenders' creative impulses.

When Prohibition began, all outlets selling liquor became speakeasies. Saloons, which had never been popular venues, were no longer legal. The licensing system became moot since alcohol was banned entirely.

Organized criminals ran the speakeasies, taking control of a racket that had before been dominated by political bosses. Pittsburgh has always had a hint of corruption, but during Prohibition it went to new levels.

Wylie Avenue was filled with theaters, dance halls and clever bartenders. The neighborhood had an influx of black southerners pouring into it to work in the mills and other industrial centers following World War I. With them came the tastes cultivated in the South. Wylie became known as Pittsburgh's Harlem.

The drinks in the Hill District reflected that. A collection of master mixologists came to dominate the nightlife in the area. Eddie Thomas became the most well-known bartender for the next few decades. He and the others would take a cue from the creative musicians and artists who visited the clubs.

The *Pittsburgh Courier* often touted the best bartenders in the area and held an annual contest for determining the best barmaids and bartenders in the city. Thomas was the perennial winner when the paper would run contests following Prohibition. He and other bartenders became heroes in the community because of their creativity and central position within the entertainment centers during the national alcohol ban and afterward. And cocktails, along with moonshine, were the popular form of drink.

Some of the Hill District establishments became known as black-and-tan clubs. Whites from other areas came to listen to jazz while dancing with the locals. Black culture spread to the whiter areas as a result.

Despite the popularity of speakeasies on Wylie, there remained a push among religious leaders in the Hill District for enforcement of the law.

Reverend A.V. Hightower, a black minister, charged in a sermon that the Hill was wide open and that police were doing nothing to cope with the evil vice. The cops called him into the station after his accusations and confronted him with various warrants on charges he was wanted on. They told him to stop his cleanup.

One effort was depicted comically in the *Pittsburgh Post-Gazette* in 1928:

> "So you say there's a speakeasy operating right next door to the Center Avenue Police Station," said Director of Public Safety James M. Clark to Hightower. "Well you see, reverend, we can't do anything on those complaints unless we get the evidence. But I'll get you a report on this."
>
> "So you want evidence director, look," the reverend said, slamming a bottle on the director's desk.
>
> "There's your moonshine director," said Hightower.
>
> The reverend then placed a map of the speakeasies in the Hill District on the table.
>
> The director sent officers to check on the bars. They came back with bottles and reported their findings.
>
> "Are you sure that's mooney?" one of the officers suggested.
>
> "Yes, are you sure that's mooney?" echoed another officer and Clark.

William "Woogie" Harris playing a mirrored piano and singing into a microphone on a raised stage in Continental bar in Crawford Grill No. 1, with bartender Tom West in background. *Charles Teenie Harris, American, 1908–98, 1945–46, Pittsburgh; photograph © 2016 Carnegie Museum of Art, Pittsburgh, Charles "Teenie" Harris Archive.*

Before anyone could stop him, the reverend opened the cork and the room filled with the smell of alcohol.

"We'll have it analyzed and see if it's liquor."

Though public officials denied that it was a wide-open city, all the neighborhoods were rife with speakeasies, brothels and gambling venues. The underworld element was calling the shots during Prohibition, which resulted in a lot more murder and violence.

The thirsty were provided with whatever they liked after the leaders of booze rings told them the "politicians had squashed everything."

Temperance organizations like the Ministerial Union, a group comprising five hundred ministers of the city, reported the conditions of the speakeasies to the police.

Police officers and city officials had been connected with the booze traffickers and charged with corruption and taking bribes. One Prohibition officer, E.C. Yellowley, promised to make the city as "dry as a Victorian novel." When the newspapers asked whether Pittsburgh was the wettest city in America, Yellowley wouldn't say if that was true or not.

The speakeasies understood they couldn't independently make moonshine. They had to buy it from official sources. If they failed to buy it from the bootleggers, the police would raid them. One man was given a $50 refund from a $100 fine after he explained to South Side police that he bought his whiskey from an "official" mooney wholesaler.

Drinking was also dangerous sport. A batch of moonshine known as Jamaica Ginger took the lives of many drinkers. In October 1923, the body of one man was found on a sidewalk on Frankstown Avenue. Another was found on the Twenty-Second Street Bridge, another on the bank of the Monongahela riverbank and another on Noblestown Road. Yet another body was found in the yard of a McKeesport mill. One person even fell dead in a suburban restaurant. Jamaica Ginger was suspected to have caused all the deaths.

"If other considerations will not stop the recklessness that drinks everything offered to it in the name of beverage, the thought—if intelligence is brought into use—that the potion may mean death or blindness ought to have its effect," the *Daily Post* said in an editorial. "Let those who have been risking their lives or their sight by drinking 'Hooch' think of the dead human bodies that were found lying around the streets from it the other day."

Pittsburgh's North Side was a lawless place. Many prostitutes worked the speakeasy circuit in the neighborhood. The Delmont Café, a cabaret operated by Joseph A. Rubin, was the most notorious bar on the North Side. It catered to college boys and young people from fine families. It was a vicious dive of the worst kind, according to the *Daily Post*.

The popularity of cocktails and Prohibition writers soared in the city during the alcohol ban. In the Hill District, Chester L. Washington became popular as a columnist for the *Courier*, as did John L. Clark. The newspaper would continue its tradition of covering the service industry throughout its existence.

Among white communities, Charles Danver was the biggest columnist in town and the one who has left the largest accounts of what its cocktail culture was like during Prohibition and the decades thereafter. He worked for the *Pittsburgh Post-Gazette*, and he became beloved for his colorful descriptions of speakeasies, clubs, cocktails and bartenders throughout his more than forty-year career. His column was known as "Pittsburghesque."

In one column, Danver told of a skyscraper speakeasy downtown. It was accessible only by private elevator, and you had to have a ticket to get to the top. The proprietor of the speakeasy reportedly put $25,000 into it. Patrons rode up in an elevator, and at the top, there was a peephole to check on passengers before they got off. The ones who were suspected of being the law were sent back down the elevator, according to Danver.

Two bartenders were behind the long, polished bar. There were slot machines, a barbecue grill and other paraphernalia common to such places. All kinds of drinks were obtainable. Stepping into it was like going to Europe, only wetter. Among the customers, there were prominent members of society, and it was one of the safest emporiums in town.

Pittsburgh attracted a great deal of industrial barons who had traveled extensively over the years. When they came back from those trips, they would bring with them cocktail recipes they'd had while away. It was another influence on the drinks made in the city.

Charles Danver was an iconic newspaperman in Pittsburgh for close to four decades, writing about bars, drinks and colorful figures in the city's nightlife. *Photo courtesy of the* Pittsburgh Post-Gazette.

On Fifth Avenue, Newell's was one of the hot spots during Prohibition. It was known from coast to coast as a rendezvous point for prizefighters, politicians and big-money sports players.

John L. Sullivan, James J. "Gentleman Jim" Corbett and such sporting celebrities were sometimes seen there. The Antler, a couple doors away, was another sparkling oasis. And the Fort Pitt hotel bar was another popular spot. Kramer's Atlantic Gardens on Diamond Street was popular among actors, musicians and politicians.

At the intermissions of the Gayety, the Bijou and the Alvin Theaters, patrons streamed into a place across the street called Tom Truby's. Anticipating the theater rush, the bartenders would have the bar lined with beers already drawn.

The William Penn Hotel in Pittsburgh had a booming speakeasy during Prohibition. The hotel remains an important part of the city's culture. *Photo courtesy Omni William Penn Hotel.*

High-salaried stage stars and jazz-world celebrities would make their best, but unadvertised, personal appearances in obscure little night haunts flourishing behind doors with peep holes. A guest list of several could have been a "who's who in the bright lights."

The entrepreneur of one hidden café boasted that in his time he had entertained such top-notchers as Al Jolson, Ted Healy, Fanny Brice, Ted

Lewis, Helen Morgan and George Dewey Washington. Occasionally, they would be prevailed on to do a song or dance at the club.

Danver discussed the fancy mixed drinks that had been popular during and before Prohibition in Pittsburgh in one column. Ginger ale highballs made with scotch or rye were the favorites. Beer was in high demand. The other drinks on the top of the list were the dry martini, Manhattan and clover club cocktails. He then went on to elaborate on the lengthy menu for the estimated 450 speakeasies in the city:

> *We don't mean to say that every oasis in Pittsburgh has such an extensive list—as a matter of fact, two or three don't—but the following cocktails, highballs, lemonades and throat gargles are obtainable at the given prices:*
> *Bacardi, 75 cents, Clover Club, 75 cents; Horse's Neck, $1.50; Pousse Café, $1.75; Dry Martini, 75 cents; Manhattan, 75 cents; Bronx, 75 cents; Orange Blossom, 75 cents; Silver Fizz, $1; Golden Fizz, $1; Gin Rickey, 50 cents; Gin Buck, 50 cents; Whisky Sour, 75 cents; Pink Lady, $1.25…*

The William Penn Hotel Lobby was booming during the city's industrial heyday. Industrial barons from all over the world came to do business and then drink in Pittsburgh. *Photo courtesy Omni William Penn Hotel.*

The bartenders during Prohibition were innovative and experimental. They were reminiscent of the upscale bartenders today who know hundreds of recipes. One ritzy East End speakeasy was said to have nearly two hundred fancy drinks on its refreshment list along with a liveried butler.

Spaghetti joints were scattered all throughout the town. They were urban institutions that were also jazz palaces and speakeasies. Spaghetti was just one feature.

Italian food dominated the city from the South Side to the North Side and the Hill District, which was deemed its native habitat. Washington Street had its spaghetti row—boxlike restaurants lined up one after the other, each boasting the best in town. They served drinks, cocktails and beer in these establishments.

Older waiters from Diamond cafés became rare in the leisurely new cafés. Café work, with high-end waiters, suffered because of the speakeasy culture. The older ones left the business.

"A waiter has to be a young man," a restaurateur told Charles Danver. "He has to have a smile. When he gets old, he's no good as a waiter any

Diamond Street was, from Prohibition into the 1950s, the place to socialize in Pittsburgh. Diamond cafés featured all sorts of drinks and all sorts of people. *Photo courtesy Carnegie Library of Pittsburgh.*

more. He has debts, his children don't turn out right, and he has a lot of worries. Then he gets a job as a night watchman."

Some aristocrats from Europe came to Pittsburgh and became waiters. A downtown hotel had a waiter who was reputed to be a former Austrian nobleman. When the crowned heads of his native land tumbled, he first went for Paris. And there, before coming to America, he earned his living by playing piano in cafés of Montmartre.

One Pittsburgh service worker was a lieutenant in the German military during the war. Richard Ditt, twenty-eight-year-old scion of a wealthy German family, attended the University of Heidelberg. He had no need for a job, so he pursued his love for music and the sciences.

Minor celebrities of sorts were frequently found in the obscurity of café kitchens and in the ranks of others administering to the wants of restaurant patrons. A chef of a downtown hotel cooked for President Woodrow Wilson on his famous trip to France aboard the *George Washington*. In a cabaret, the eats were prepared by one who once ruled the kitchens of Italian nobility. In a downtown chop suey temple, a young Chinese man who once was employed in the same capacity by the Vanderbilts purchased the food.

The bottom eventually fell out under everyone. The stock market crash began on October 24, 1929. It was known as Black Thursday. The cataclysm was the start of the Great Depression and the end of the Roaring Twenties.

People made a run on the banks. Many were out of work, and the festive ambience of speakeasies took on a more somber mood. Speakeasy proprietors had to change their approach to selling alcohol. In Pittsburgh on New Year's Eve 1929, there was the sound of popping corks, hysterical whistles and patrol wagon bells, as told by Danver. The revelers opted to sing "Sweet Adeline," a sobering tune, instead of the New Year's staple "Auld Lang Syne."

In all the roadhouses, speakeasies and hotels, Prohibition agents were temporarily blind and joy was unconfined.

The nightclub proprietors asked drinkers to not laugh when they placed cards on the table. Many people went to church instead for night services. And the somber mood extended throughout the effort at economic recovery. There was a speakeasy near the Webster Avenue lodging house that gave a free drink to each job seeker in the morning. At 6:00 a.m., there was a lineup of fifty to sixty unfortunates. All were waiting for the woman who ran the place to give them an eye-opener. The free drink gave them the courage to go panhandling for the day. The proprietress of the speakeasy knew they would spend most of their money at her bar at which they gathered at the end of the day.

Competition was keen among speakeasies during the Depression. They brought in feature stunts to attract business. Musicians were a popular choice.

The entrance to a certain speakeasy was in an alley in which a restaurant discarded its unwanted food. Daily beggars would visit the place and pretend to be starving and dig into the refuse cans. Patrons of the speakeasy saw this and came through with a quarter or a half dollar. The alleged victims of starvation profited handsomely.

When the Great Depression and Prohibition coincided, it was an interesting point in the city. Speakeasies were known as places of high times, but the streets were full of beggars. The paradox of Pittsburgh at the time showed when people would visit their favorite oasis.

Despite the hardship, the speakeasy trade was an attractive one for people to undertake. While other jobs were scarce, it seemed that bartenders and bar proprietors were making enough money to support families. The highest-paid bartender in 1931 Pittsburgh was employed in an East End establishment, from which he collected $125 a week. The next-highest paid was employed downtown and found $100 in the little envelope each Saturday. The amount included a predetermined "cut" or bonus for willingness on the part of the drink dispenser to "take the rap" in case of a raid. Ordinarily, a Pittsburgh bartender was paid around $60 a week.

The trade's appeal eventually made it harder for speakeasies to survive because so many people started them. One closed in 1931 because the owner couldn't pay the rent. A number of proprietors went out soliciting business. Another blow to the craft cocktail movement was the influx of people into the profession who were beginners. They had not mastered the list of cocktails that their predecessors had. These people didn't know how to make the same types of drinks, but they saw the profitability of operating speakeasies. Still, there were those who could make the difficult Pousse Café, which was known as the hardest to mix. One bartender told Danver in 1932 that he was able to make fifty-four different drinks.

In that same year, a booklet of cocktail recipes called *Bottoms Up* was released and published in Pittsburgh. Its highball recipes included Special Soul Kiss, Tip Top Bracer, Silver Dream, Snowball, Golden Dream, Tom and Jerry, Jersey Lily, Pousse Café, Mamie Taylor–Southern Style, Peach Blow, Widow's Kiss and Widow's Kiss No. 2.

Speakeasy operators undertook innovative ways to attract new customers during the Depression. The proprietors would send out "shills" to bring in business. They would encourage people to enter the bars and grab a drink. It was an early form of marketing. The shills were usually the bartenders who weren't busy making drinks. Pittsburgh speakeasies began offering free lunches to bait people on certain nights of the week to attract visitors. The return of the free lunch began a few years before with a platter of microscopic cheese cubes and crackers at the end of the bar, according to Danver. It was originally a show of the proprietor's magnanimity or conscientiousness. It developed into a vital economic factor in the speakeasy business.

Speakeasy proprietors had to come up with new features. There were tables for ladies, jazz bands, singing waiters, card tables and nickel photographs and radios. They enlarged the free lunch. Soup became an added attraction. One place put in an electric toaster for hot dogs, but another place quickly outdid that by offering each patron who desired it a hard-boiled egg. One joint had a chef who sliced cold pork.

Some of the hard-pressed speakeasies were using mailing lists and telephone directories to drum up business. Patrons were notified of special "free lunches," which in those desperate days amounted to sumptuous spreads. One place offered a seafood dinner. Another made beef stew to compete with it.

Many discovered it was impossible to maintain a high-class place without losing money.

The free dinner was the next big thing. Some establishments gave potato salad, sliced ham, spaghetti, baked beans and hot dogs with sliced tomatoes. Chili con carne and other comestibles were also offered.

Some of the big shots in the organized syndicate who were supposed to be cut in weren't satisfied with beer sales. There were several places that couldn't pay their beer bills, being $300 to $500 behind. Eventually, the bootleggers and organized criminals wanted fewer speakeasies and better salesmanship.

Because of the economic hardships, police were less vigilant in placing people behind bars for trying to make money through liquor sales. A man who had seven kids owned one place that was raided. The Prohibition agents' reaction was telling about how difficult economically the times were. Federal agents came in and started breaking bottles when one man told him, "Listen, Mac—you wouldn't have to knock off this place if you didn't want to, would you? This poor guy just opened up and hasn't gotten a nickel. He's been out of work for six months and has a wife and seven kids to support. You could forget about it if you wanted to, couldn't you?"

The agent put down the second bottle without smashing it.

"How do I know he has seven kids?" he retorted. "Anyhow I have to make report on this place when I get back to the office."

"Well you could say you didn't find anything, couldn't you? And if you want to see the kids, they live across the street."

After conferring with his partner, the agent stepped out of the place and crossed the street. When he returned he nodded, saying, "Yeah, there's seven all right. And it looks as if they hadn't eaten for a week."

The police officers decided to bust a place down the street and permit the man to continue selling the brew, according to the *Pittsburgh Post-Gazette*.

There remained those who enjoyed revelry late into the night and early into the morning. Some speakeasies got bouncing at 6:00 a.m. to 7:00 a.m. with the people who stayed out all night wanting to continue into the morning.

One of Pittsburgh's streets was known as Rum Row because it was so famous for the amount of drinking undertaken there. There was a legend that a certain Pittsburgher spent most of $25,000 on Rum Row traveling from one oasis to the next. Eventually, Rum Row proprietors were so greedy for customers that their shills dragged in Prohibition agents, getting all the bars closed down.

Fifth Avenue, Pittsburgh's main strip, was a shadow of what it was in the Roaring Twenties.

"Something's happened to the Avenue," policeman Dick Currie told Charles Danver. "It's lost its color. The people seem to go home earlier. And you don't see the old crowds that made it their hangout. Even the college boys have quieted down and stopped cutting capers."

Black-and-tan clubs, which once lured white people into black haunts for something well heeled, became a thing of the past. The Hill District had one or two spots where black and white people could mingle on the dance floor. But they didn't get much patronage in the Depression. They would eventually become popular during the economic recovery years later.

Home parties became the way people celebrated. They stayed in instead of going to bars or cafés.

In 1932, the push for repeal heightened. Mob bosses, who had made a fortune during Prohibition, weren't happy. But people who wanted higher-quality alcohol and beer welcomed it. Speakeasy owners got restless when the advent of legalized beer approached again. Some told a reporter they didn't know whether to laugh or cry over the return of legal brew. They were worried about legislation controlling their working hours, which they felt would tell them they couldn't operate past midnight. They also thought it would be hard to get licenses if they had been raided at one time.

Beer, while bringing back good fellowship, had also brought the bootlegging industry its greatest depression since Prohibition. Those who sold beer legally made a great deal more money. One place that used to make $200 a night made $2,200 a night selling the good beer. Legal beer was sold in restaurants.

By 1933, Rum Row, which once featured eight speakeasies, had but one lonely oasis, and it was on the verge of closing. A former customer said, "With all the thugs at large, who wants to go into alleys these nights?" Rum Row, in the shadow of the Pitt Theater, would be torn down to make room for a parking lot in 1934.

The racketeers and bootleggers who had made money continued to make money on the sale of beer by paying for the licenses of people who had been speakeasy proprietors.

With the onset of the Depression and end of Prohibition came the end of an era and the colorful, Wild West feel of the city of Pittsburgh. Hard liquor came back in November 1933 as a legal form of spirit with the repeal of Prohibition nationally. The speakeasies took it a little sadly. After the vote to make repeal complete, there were crowds in most of the speakeasies—and

Real beer was in popular demand when Prohibition ended. The Oyster House was filled with patrons when the ban on alcohol was lifted. *Photo courtesy of the Oyster House.*

even some customers were mourning the passage of what would be considered the good old days.

"Yes we're going to have legal liquor and drinking won't be a social obligation anymore, it'll just be a bad habit," one customer told a *Post-Gazette* reporter.

"Straight liquor" was sold for fifteen to fifty cents and cocktails from thirty-five to seventy-five cents, and there was nothing old-fashioned about them except the names.

Local and state officials also targeted speakeasies for raids after Prohibition to enforce license laws. Restaurants, cocktail lounges and cafés became the new places for people to drink.

Repeal went over big on Wylie Avenue, according to the *Pittsburgh Courier*.

"It came as if to stimulate a sagging 'spirits' of the 'Street of streets,'" the newspaper said. "It came as a hopeful herald of better times. Lights flared…a milling crowd shifted to and fro…the novel noise of clicking glasses and soothing strains of syncopated music sifted through the crevices of countless doorways.…And powdered faces passed like ships in the night.…This was the Avenue's welcome for the homecoming of Old John Barleycorn."

The time of the speakeasy had passed.

"Repeal was slowly becoming the established order in Pittsburgh restaurants and hotels yesterday, with no evidence at all that the death knell of prohibition was to be marked by anything resembling a lengthy spree," the *Post-Gazette* said in a December 7, 1933 article. "On the streets, there was no indication that a unique era had passed away—but there was plenty of evidence in cafes and dining rooms."

Pittsburghesque Cocktail

Named after Charles Danver's famous Pittsburgh newspaper column, this cocktail was popular at many cafés and speakeasies, each of which put its own spin on it.

1 ounce Beefeater Gin
½ ounce blackberry-infused cognac (recipe follows)
½ ounce banana-infused Old Overholt Rye Whiskey (recipe follows)
½ ounce cream
¼ ounce simple syrup

When building cocktails, both shaken and stirred, it's important to add ingredients in order from least expensive to most expensive. If you make a mistake, it's better to throw out a tin of juice and start over again than it is to have to dispose of 2 ounces of expensive liquor because some eggshell got into the mix. So, with that in mind, build your cocktail in the shorter shaker tin, then add ice. Regular bar ice works. Fill the shaker to the top. Place the taller tin over the short one and give it a firm tap to seal. The taller tin should seal onto the shorter tin at a 20-degree angle. It needs to be tight enough so you can lift both contacted tins from the base of the taller tin. Shake the cocktail. Using a Hawthorne strainer, strain the cocktail through a fine mesh tea strainer into a chilled coupe glass. With a double-strain method, you don't need to worry about an overabundance of ice chips in your cocktail, as the fine mesh strainer will capture all of them as well as fruit or other leafy detritus that you may have in your shaker.

Blackberry-Infused Cognac
1 pint fresh blackberries
750-milliliter bottle preferred cognac

Muddle blackberries. Add cognac. Infuse for 24 hours. Strain out berries using a cheesecloth or coffee filter.

Banana-Infused Old Overholt Rye Whiskey
3 bananas, peeled and sliced
750-milliliter bottle Old Overholt Rye Whiskey

Combine bananas and rye. Infuse for 3 days.

3

CAFÉS AND JAZZ CLUBS

In the immediate decades following Prohibition, two bartenders with Cuban ties arrived in Pittsburgh and brought with them a Caribbean view of cocktail making.

Among them was Jack Davis, wine steward at the Roosevelt Hotel, who was the chief mixologist at Sloppy Joe's, an influential bar in Havana where the daiquiri was refined by native bartenders. Havana was a hot spot for American celebrities, including Ernest Hemingway.

Joe Sala, another Cuban bartender and perhaps the most influential in the city, worked at the Sixth Avenue Café and other places throughout his long career in Pittsburgh. While in Cuba, Sala had served Douglas Fairbanks, both senior and junior; the Gish sisters; and Charlie Chaplin.

Sala was born in Havana and apprenticed at the ritzier places there. During Prohibition, he made cocktails for Americans, including Mary Pickford, and dreamed of one day owning a bar in the United States.

He made a mark when he arrived in Pittsburgh. Sala knew the favorite drinks of two hundred Pittsburghers before their order. He invented several drinks, including the Willows Fizz and the Tequila Pancho, a sledgehammer drink made of Mexican whiskey.

Sala was Charles Danver's favorite bartender and was occasionally mentioned in the "Pittsburghesque" column. He became a society figure who was gossiped about.

Shortly after the daiquiri arrived in America, its first mention appeared in *Post-Gazette* accounts of what drinks were the most popular in the city.

Sala Steps Out on His Own

JOE SALA   MRS. TONY CONFORTI
—Post-Gazette Photo.
For 14 years, or ever since he came to Pittsburgh from Havana, Sala has worked for Tony Conforti at the Nixon Cafe. Last night Sala opened his own night club, El Chico, a Spanish-type spot, in the Plaza Cafe and on hand to wish him luck was the only boss he's ever had in Pittsburgh. Here is the wife of his former employer echoing her husband's sentiments at El Chico's formal opening.

Joe Sala was one of the city's most important historic figures in bartending. He brought a Cuban flair and taste to the craft while here in the 1930s, 1940s and 1950s. *Photo courtesy of the* Pittsburgh Post-Gazette.

Though arguments over the daiquiri's origin prevail among cocktail experts, Sala and Davis are the most likely people to have introduced it to the Greater Pittsburgh area. This goes against the perception that the great cocktail trends start on the coast and filter inward.

Other classic drinks remained popular in the city after repeal. Whiskey sours were a favorite drink in Pittsburgh. Bartenders attested at the time that the Manhattan was the most popular, followed by the old-fashioned. Side cars were a hit, martinis were popular as always and, in Cuban fashion, the Bacardi cocktail was also another one sipped by the elbow-benders. Tom Collinses also came into vogue. Danver's rising popularity led three or four places to create Pittsburghesque cocktails. Danver said there were so many cocktails being made that they were hard up for names to give them on their menus.

Names for drinks came from names seen in the newspaper, whether it was columnists or public figures. In the 1930s, the proprietor of the Triangle Café urged friends who expected to drive to stick to "Musmanno Highballs," which were plain ginger ale. The drink was named after a judge in the area who was harsh on drunk drivers.

Cafés on Diamond Street were among the most fashionable places to visit in the years immediately following Prohibition. The Diamond cafés were often high-end establishments that businessmen visited for after-work cocktails. It was a place where wealth was exhibited or feigned.

One of the greatest poseurs of the era on Diamond Street was Colonel T. Hemingway McInerny. He wore wing collars, phony diamonds, a lapel carnation and spats and carried a gold-headed cane he said came from J.J. McGraw, the longtime manager of the New York Giants.

He usually dined with friends or as a guest of the proprietor. He would present the waiter with ten or twenty dollars and declare loudly that they keep the change.

Before leaving, he would get the waiter aside and demand the soft money. When he died, his wealth amounted to one dime.

In the '30s, Diamond Street's neon-lit crowds overflowed the sidewalks. Owners faced fierce competition in that neighborhood. They offered great deals on food and drink to draw in customers who would go elsewhere without the deals.

River Avenue was a venue for lovers. Couples would go there and spoon or hold hands in the shadows of Schenley Park's Circle and on the benches of West Park. One of the bright spots along the avenue was a houseboat, café and club in which jazz music played in the late hours.

The North Side remained a Wild West scene. Danver said it brought to mind frontier dance halls since there was such a disparity in the getups worn by men. They wore everything from tuxedos to lumberjack coats and tassel caps.

While the swanky cafés attracted posh crowds in the '30s, numerous dives were clustered in lower-income neighborhoods.

Anything went in these places. Smells of beer, cigars, cheap perfume and body odor mingled to give it a unique atmosphere.

The only thing that wasn't permitted was to gaze too long on another man's girl, or you might be punched in the face. The stretches of streets where these places were located were dubbed the Barbary Coast.

When Prohibition ended, some speakeasies became known as "one-man clubs," a phrase that came about because the revenues fell into the pocket of one man. These after-hour clubs served liquor between 2:00 a.m. and 7:00 a.m., as well as on Sundays. By 1936, more than six hundred one-man clubs existed.

The cocktail hour for most people was at 5:00 p.m., when work let out. But between 3:00 a.m. and 5:00 a.m., musicians, hotel workers, chorus girls, newspapermen and other night workers dropped into their favorite spots for a drink and song. The lies they told weren't as polite, nor was the lovemaking.

Drinkers mingled with the entertainment. Some of the musicians were forced to drink cocktails with customers.

"They insist that you have a cocktail with them, and you can't get out of it," one musician said to the *Post-Gazette*. "If you refuse, the management gets sore, and you can't get away with tea anymore because they bring the stuff in glasses. The result is, there's hardly a morning I don't go home talking to myself."

In the 1940s, after-hour clubs in the Hill District were important parts of the nightlife, according to a dissertation by Colter Harper, a musician who wrote a history of the jazz era in Pittsburgh. They were run as social clubs, which enabled them to evade the laws restricting hours of operation. The Musicians' Club was one after-hours organization. The Bambola Club was another. Jazz was a big part of the experience at these places.

Shake dancers, female impersonators and raucous music were all part of the experience for people who patronized or were members of the clubs.

The Cotton Club, run by A.C. Harris and bartended by Ernie Bossie, earned a reputation as a premier cocktail spot in the Hill District.

The bartenders who perennially finished atop the *Pittsburgh Courier*'s best bartender list included Bossie. The others in the Hill District usually named were Eddie Thomas, Jim Banks, Asa Harris, Oscar James, Charlie Williams, Tom West and Cal Butler.

Three men—including bartender Ernest Bossie, *center*, wearing a zippered cardigan and a holding cigar—gathered at a bar with boxing pictures and a sign reading "please pay when served," in Silver Bar and Grill, 1911, Centre Avenue. *Charles Teenie Harris, American, 1908–98, 1945–46, Pittsburgh; photograph © 2016 Carnegie Museum of Art, Pittsburgh, Charles "Teenie" Harris Archive.*

The Crawford Grill produced some of Pittsburgh's great bartenders. Under the tutelage of Eddie Thomas, and with jazz inspiring them, they would foster a tradition of excellence in bartending. Emerson (Pete) Peterson was one mixologist who came out of the Crawford Grill.

Teenie Harris, the famous photographer for the *Courier*, visited the bars in the neighborhood to capture the jazz environment. The savvy of the mixologists was occasionally mentioned in his photo captions.

Tom West, who worked at Javo's Jungle, lorded over a futuristic bar in the 1930s while his fame grew, according to a 1935 *Pittsburgh Courier* article. West could make anything, from a Bacardi cocktail to a brandy julep or Pousse Café.

"He knows his cocktails, his fizzes, his rickeys, his sours, his punches and Champagne like nobody's business, and he has everything in his bar to make you anything you can imagine," the *Courier* wrote.

Some of the black bartenders in the 1930s Hill District were overly confident. Al Williams, barkeep at Jimmie's Tavern on Herron Avenue, said he would buy any drinks for a person who requested something he couldn't make.

Women were largely waitresses and had to endure "barroom Romeos" while they served drinks. Elizabeth Quarrels, better known as "Mickey," worked at the Crawford Grill. "I can hardly restrain myself from using profane language or taking a punch at some of the men we term as cuties," she told the *Courier*. "The fellow that gets a few drinks under his belt and thinks the waitress should spend her time listening to his cute remarks and attempts to date her up."

Female bartenders made a mark in Pittsburgh. Arnetta Green was the chief barmaid at Ernie Bossie's place on East Wylie. There was a bid for her services before she selected Bossie's establishment as the place of her employment. "Net," as Green was called, was considered the best among female mixologists in the neighborhood.

Despite their expertise, black bartenders encountered racism from unions and white establishments when applying for memberships or positions. Sam Haney, a bartender and part-time cook at Yellin Grill on Wylie Avenue, applied to join the Bartenders Union Local 188 in 1941. The Union was not receptive to his application. "The time is not ripe to make any effort to get Negroes into the Bartender's Union," said Robert Daley, president. "The boys don't want them in and that just about settles everything." The union also told Haney that he would be unable to apply for any union membership if his application were rejected. Haney would have to undergo a rigorous test to join the union as well. Haney told them he would take the test whenever they wanted him to.

Pittsburgh started to come out of the Depression at the beginning of the 1940s. The amount of business done on the North Side, South Side and downtown in that time amazed Danver. He described it as an air of gaiety among the crowds gathered there.

The tone of newspaper archives became upbeat, though the prospect of war was on the horizon.

Some ritzy places were established in the city. Joe Sala opened El Chico, an upscale bar that attracted Billy Conn, a prominent boxer, among other people.

Bill Green's Casino and Terraced Gardens in Pleasant Hills on Route 51 was another hub of Pittsburgh's nightlife from the 1930s into the 1950s. It booked nationally known performers in the big-band era and was known for its quality service.

The Bachelor's Club on Penn Avenue in East Liberty boasted a prominent clientele that was surprised by a police raid in 1941. The *Post-Gazette*'s front-page story reported the police detained 129 people, 40 of whom were women; seized $1,500 worth of choice liquors; and found evidence of gambling. The club had no liquor license. It took state police equipped with sledgehammers fifteen minutes to break down the six steel doors leading into the club.

Other venues in the East End during the 1940s included Lepus, Hunting and Fishing and the Del Mar Canoe Club, which offered after-hours gambling and featured some of the best comedians in the country.

The downtown area included the Variety Club, Chelsea, Almono, the Musicians' Club and the Benjamin Harrison Literary Club, which was an after-hours spot on Liberty Avenue that was supposedly owned by gangsters, according to a retrospective written by Nate Guidry for the *Post-Gazette*.

The North Side featured clubs such as Red's Cafe, Pace's and the Moose Club.

The greater part of 1941 was a good time for all who wanted to drink in the city.

Then Pearl Harbor happened. The bombing sobered the city, and with the declaration of war later on in 1941, the city began looking overseas.

The New Year's Eve celebration after Pearl Harbor was a strange cocktail of orchids and champagne, comparative sobriety and patriotic songs, as Danver described it. Nightclubs had orderly crowds. One bar closed each floorshow with "God Bless America."

At several downtown clubs, ladies wore Hawaiian leis of gardenias and camellias to show support for the victims of the Japanese attack.

Many would sing, "Heigh-ho, heigh-ho, to Tokyo we'll go—to bomb the Japs."

Public officials proposed nighttime curfews as a wartime measure. Cabaret owners thought it would be the end of business. The Retail Liquor Dealers Association, which wanted defense workers in the city to feel like going to their jobs in the morning, supported the measure.

Bars exhibited patriotism by changing their names. Smithfield Street's former German Kitchen became the Victory Bar and Grill. And the Allies Café across the street put an illuminated red, white and blue *V* in its window.

Service industry workers were drafted just the same as every other class.

In March 1942, at the Gay Nineties just before midnight, there was a phone call for the club's pianist, Dorothy Nesbit. At the end of her song, she took the phone. When she returned, she looked blue, and there were tears in her eyes.

One after another, waiters and waitresses went to the phone. The bartender was the last one to talk. The conversation was brief for each one, and they returned with solemn faces.

The call was from their former headwaiter, Alex DiCroce. It was revealed that he was due to sail the next morning to an unknown destination in service to the country. He'd spent about a month's pay phoning from the West Coast to tell his old friends.

During the war, bartenders and elbow-benders honored war heroes. The Commando Kelly was a cocktail named after Medal of Honor winner Charles E. Kelly, who hailed from Pittsburgh. The drink had a double shot of gin, one shot of crème de menthe and a splash of grenadine.

Toward the end of the war, nightclub business boomed. According to some reports, it picked up fivefold. People were spending much more money at bars.

One drink that was favored by sailors at home on leave was the Depth Bomb, which consisted of a glass of beer and a shot of liquor, glass and all, submerged. Quickly downed, the immediate effect was a sharp click of the shot glass on their front teeth.

The William Penn Hotel was another hot spot for drinkers in the wartime years. George Kokinakas, a twenty-five-year service industry veteran who referred to himself as "the one and only George," worked at the basement bar of the William Penn Hotel. He drew his name from the motto "the customer is *never* right," which he felt made him unique. George told the *Post-Gazette* in 1945:

> *I've seen 'em come and I've seen 'em go, and believe me, I don't bow to no one. The women are really the two-fisted drinkers these days. They don't care what the hell they drink, as long as it's got alcohol in it. But I can tell by their eyes. I can tell a woman's age by her eyes too. I usually cut off their drinks (And they almost always drink mixed ones) and if they get tough I just give them one too many and let the house dick take over from there.*

He recommended a hangover cure for those who went too hard. It was called the Morning Glory Feast. It was the juice of one lemon, the white of an egg, a shot of scotch, a teaspoonful of sugar, two dashes of absinthe and charged water, all shaken well and served in a ten-ounce glass. The drink was copyrighted.

The reverence for President Franklin Delano Roosevelt was great in the city. So his death in 1945 was met with a somber mood from nightlife workers.

William Penn bartender George Kokinakas's skill in making drinks was matched by his charm. He believed the customer was "never right." *Photo courtesy of the* Pittsburgh Post-Gazette.

When news of his passing went through the cafés and diners, patrons looked up in disbelief and thought it was a joke. When they found out it was true, they muttered words of surprise and regret before returning to their drinks with pondering faces. Bartenders moodily washed their glasses, as described by Danver. Those who were loud fell silent. Business fell 50 percent in some places, and most of the customers were strangers instead of regulars. They felt as if their father had passed away. Waiters cried over the news.

The five years following the war were a big transition for the service industry. Pittsburgh earned a reputation as a shot and beer town beginning in the 1950s. A number of factors would reinforce that perception over the coming decades. The first trigger was suburban flight.

When the men returned from World War II, they didn't want to live in the downtown area. They wanted to go to the suburbs. Pittsburgh, as it now stands, is much more sprawling in its population than it was during its speakeasy era.

With fewer people came a drop-off in business in the city's bars.

The suburban bars had more of a welcoming type of feel. It was, and is, more like a family for the customer and bartenders who drink there. And it is also, as a drawback, less like a lab for experimenting with drinks.

Another thing that hurt the craft cocktail trade was the banning of female bartenders in Pennsylvania beginning in 1941. The ban lasted until 1967. Women had been an influential force in bars for nearly half a century in Pittsburgh. Preventing half of the population from engaging in the profession limited the amount of innovation that bartenders would undertake.

In the Hill District, the golden era of jazz, creative cocktails and artistic endeavors would continue throughout the 1950s and 1960s. Places like Birdie's Hurricane were popular.

As the *Post-Gazette* put it, "The Hurricane whirled and thundered with the acutest minds and the biggest hearts in the world of jazz. The Ellingtons, the Basies and the Vaughans came to call and the Elbridges, the George Bensons, the Roland Kirks, the Wild Bill Davises and the Nancy Wilsons came to make music."

As was established for the rest of Pittsburgh's nightlife history, music and innovative drink making went hand in hand.

It was said that Anna Simmons Dunlap, known as Birdie and owner of the place, was descended from Sally Hemings, who was President Thomas Jefferson's mistress.

"There was absolutely no petting in the club or she'd put you smack out in the middle of the street," Frank Bolden, former *Pittsburgh Courier* editor,

Jazz band, with Jimmy Smith on organ, possibly Eddie McFadden on guitar and possibly Donald Bailey on drums, performing in Hurricane Club. *Charles Teenie Harris, American, 1908–98, 1953–56, Pittsburgh; photograph © 2016 Carnegie Museum of Art, Pittsburgh, Charles "Teenie" Harris Archive.*

was quoted as saying in the *Post-Gazette*. "Girls were safer at the Hurricane than at the YMCA."

The Crawford Grill remained the most important club until 1968, when Martin Luther King Jr. was assassinated. His death caused riots in the city that destroyed much of the Hill District. But up to then, the grill was important.

"The Grill was the spot," Pittsburgh pianist Walt Harper told the *Post-Gazette*. "Everyone that was someone in show business hung out at the Grill. Frank Sinatra. Nat Cole. Chico Hamilton hung out at the Grill. The place was very cosmopolitan. People could have a good time without having to worry about anything."

In downtown Pittsburgh, nightclubs such as the Copa and the Carousel, located near the Nixon Theater, were central to Pittsburgh's nightlife during the 1950s. Joe Sala worked that circuit.

Though the after-work cocktail was usually had in the suburbs, the city still maintained cocktail lounges. The bartenders there fought the perception that Pittsburgh wasn't creating interesting drinks. And amid the music of Elvis Presley, Bob Dylan and the Beatles, the alternative crowd that visited those places looked more for philosophical talk and reflective musings.

Morning Glory Feast
George Kokinakas, William Penn Hotel, 1945

This cocktail was considered a hangover cure made by William Penn Hotel bartender George Kokinakas in the 1940s. It's an obvious reproduction of the classic Morning Glory Fizz, which first appeared in George Kappeler's 1895 book **American Modern Drinks**. *This didn't stop "the one and only" George Kokinakas from claiming his own copyright in 1945.*

1 teaspoon sugar
1 ounce lemon juice
1 egg white
1 ounce Scotch whisky
2 dashes absinthe
Fill: soda water

Combine sugar and lemon juice in a mixing tin and stir until sugar melts. Add egg white, whiskey and absinthe. Shake vigorously without ice. This process is called a "dry shake," and it will give your cocktail a fuller froth and more pleasing taste. It should be a hard shake and last up to a minute, with you stopping twice during the process to break the seal and allow the gases released from the egg to escape. During this process, I watch for consistency of my liquid. I review the liquid as it drips from the top tin into the larger tin once I crack it. By the third shake, I usually have a thick stream as it passes from one tin to the next. Then I know it's done. Add ice and give the cocktail a final hard shake to chill the drink. Then the cocktail is poured straight into a Collins glass using only a Hawthorne strainer, bypassing the double strain option. You should have a beautiful, creamy, frothy, cloudy cocktail that will be light and airy to the taste. Slowly add soda water to fill glass.

4
COCKTAIL LOUNGES AND HIPPIES

When Maurice C. Dreicer, the eminent expert of cocktails, visited Pittsburgh in May 1954, he ruefully admitted to the *Post-Gazette* that he didn't know how to whip up a Puddler and Helper. The reporters told Dreicer that a Puddler and Helper was a steelworker's name for a shot of whiskey and a beer chaser.

"Oh," he said, "you mean a Boilermaker."

"I used to do a 7:30 a.m. news broadcast in New York and I always had a double bourbon, a beer and two hard-boiled eggs before every show. Had to give it up though," sighed Dreicer. "The hard-boiled eggs disagreed with me."

Dreicer at the time was the only mixologist who ever created a record with swishing sound effects that told listeners how to make cocktails. In his visits to Pittsburgh, Dreicer told the newspaper that he spent 90 percent of his time, outside of sleeping, in bars.

"I have noticed that most Pittsburghers go at drinking as if it were a quick duty, like shaving. It's that way in most industrial cities. No leisure."

While in the city, he was visited by Thomas P. Johnson, co-owner of the Pittsburgh Pirates. For Mr. Johnson, he created a Cellar cocktail, which included two jiggers of rum, one of bourbon and one of vodka in a mixing glass, along with a dash of anisette.

"Then pour a slug of straight whiskey, repeat six times and instead of a Cellar Cocktail, you'll think it's a Pennant," Dreicer said.

Comedians disparaged Pittsburgh as a place bereft of interesting alcoholic drinks in the 1950s and early 1960s. A frustrated downtown nightclub owner commented after he went out of business in the 1950s, "Pittsburgh is strictly a shot-and-a-beer town."

But professionals in Pittsburgh were cultivating and maintaining the bartending craft. The Bartenders Union Local 188 opened a six-week bartending school in 1962, with two classes a week, educating bartenders about the drinks that were popular.

The school was designed to prepare the younger members for jobs in higher-class restaurants. The professors were longtime bartenders. From a field of eighty applicants, only half were chosen. The final test was to make a difficult Pousse Café, with its five to fourteen layers of colored liqueurs.

A good cocktail could be bought in a number of neighborhoods. The area from Route 51 from the Fort Pitt Tunnels to the Elizabeth Bridge became known as Cocktail Canyon

Maurice Dreicer, eminent cocktail critic at the time, was puzzled by Pittsburghers' insistence on calling a boilermaker a "puddler" when he visited in the 1950s. *Photo courtesy of* Pittsburgh Post-Gazette.

because of the number of lounges and taverns on the stretch. By Danver's estimate, there were fifty-seven of these types of bars.

But the most interesting scene in Pittsburgh's nightlife during the late 1950s and early '60s was in Shadyside. The Casbah, in Shadyside, was the city's first intimate cocktail lounge when it opened in 1952. The owner, Eddie Edelstein, who bought it in 1957, told the *Post-Gazette* that the lounge had a demanding clientele.

"We have a customer who repeatedly sends back his martinis, complaining they are not dry enough," Edelstein said. "So one night we gave him straight gin—absolutely no vermouth. Sure enough, he sent it back. 'Won't you people ever learn to make a Dry Martini?' he said."

Cocktail lounges proliferated after Casbah opened.

In a November 1960 *Post-Gazette* article, a young Myron Cope wrote an article arguing the merits of the city's cocktail culture. By his estimate, Pittsburgh had as many cocktail lounges as most other American cities of comparable size, if not more.

"Pittsburgh's cocktail lounges, with their loveseats, their mosaic tables, their gaslight lamps, their surrealistic paintings and their abstract customers, cater to a variety of tastes," Cope wrote.

The Mecca, an Arabic waterhole that provided private cubbyholes that were entered through a beaded curtain, was among the bars listed in the article. Pretty, bare-shouldered "slave girls" served customers while they listened to Mediterranean music.

Cope mentioned the Encore in Shadyside, which he said was graced by occasional beatniks, a bearded physician who drove a motorcycle, a young man who wore a tuxedo and tennis shoes, barefoot ladies and the society leader Marjorie Merriweather Post May.

"Do your customers write on the rest room walls?" owner Will Shiner was asked.

"Oh yes," replied Shiner. "But in Latin."

Shiner grew up in Squirrel Hill. His father had a bar in the Hill District. Shiner was very close to his dad, and he inherited the attitudes developed by operating a business in a predominantly black neighborhood.

"I think what influenced him was the type of person his father was," said Lynn Shiner, Will's daughter. "I think from that standpoint, being around his father influenced him."

The Encore Lounge was one of the hippest cocktail lounges in Shadyside during the 1950s and 1960s. It was a haven for artists and beatniks. *Photo from Bill McNeil's personal collection.*

Shiner and his wife moved to Shadyside in the 1950s and saw the long lines outside Casbah. He decided to open the Encore, which became a thriving entertainment spot staffed by innovative bartenders.

"It was a wonderful musical venue," Lynn Shiner said in an interview. "There were just fine artists from all over the country who played there. It was a very lively fun place and a great venue for food and drinks. It became the neighborhood gathering spot."

Dizzy Gillespie, George Benson and Ella Fitzgerald performed at the bar.

Shadyside in the 1960s was a place of bell-bottoms, marijuana pipes and Volkswagen Bugs. The *Pittsburgh Press* called it "Our Greenwich Village."

The Encore became the most famous cocktail lounge in Pittsburgh. Most of its drinks were the classics, such as Old-Fashioneds, but the club had a number of cleverly crafted cocktails that drew inspiration from all quarters. When a State Liquor Control Board informer charged that the bar was too dimly lit, it came up with a drink called the "Insufficient Lighting Cocktail."

The Milltown was another drink served at the Encore. Mark Goldberg, drug salesman, invented it. It was made of vodka, orange juice, pineapple juice and lemon juice and served in a copper mug. The Beatnik Bender, which had Benedictine, blackberry cordial and brandy, was another one named after the spirit of the times. As Danver put it, "After several encores, you get the message man, which is to pick your beard up off the floor and make for the ol' pad."

To attract crowds for the musicians, Shiner offered a two-dollar strip steak special that came with French fries. Between the steak and labor, he was losing money. But he required a two-drink minimum. Every night, they would pack the place. Shiner was progressive in his political views, though he wasn't a hippie. He was a champion for civil rights as well. He promoted the first black bartender, Bobby Davis, in a 99 percent white club. Davis would tell the *Courier* in 1985:

[Will Shiner] *liked me so well he made me the manager. This was a time when whites would write letters saying they didn't want to rub elbows with a Black. The man was great because he gambled with his business. He won in the end.*

In my opinion, the Encore was the greatest jazz club. Even when jazz was down in NYC, we were bringing in national acts.

Davis would go on to become an influential bartender in the city for the next few decades. Among the clubs he would help operate was the Celebrity, a hot spot for black socialites in the 1980s.

Shiner had been running the jazz and hip spot for years before the hippie revolution later on in the generation, but he adapted to the times by opening a number of different establishments.

"He had a place up the street called the Pizza Pub, which had the best cheesesteaks in town," his son Jim Shiner said over the phone. "It had beer from around the world when no one else was doing that. The hippies of the '60s came in."

After closing the Pizza Pub, Shiner leased it to Froggy Morris, who reopened it as the Raspberry Rhinoceros, which was a very fashionable nightclub in the 1970s and 1980s. It was eventually replaced by a Banana Republic.

Shiner also ran the Gaslight in Shadyside in the 1960s and 1970s. It was a three-story building that had been a Roaring Twenties bar. On the main floor, there was a bar that went the whole length of the room. On

Antiwar activists and hippies would frequent the Pizza Pub, owned by Will Shiner, during the 1960s. It was a popular nightspot for them while they planned protests. *Photo from Bill McNeil's personal collection.*

the top floor, it was fine dining. It was a club, which permitted it to stay open an hour later.

"It was controversial when it first opened," Jim Shiner said. "The art in there featured nudes. The district attorney was a little put out by that and threatened prosecution. But he learned every piece in there was done by a famous European artist."

And there were plenty of cocktail lounges. Aside from the Encore and Casbah, there was Le Mardi Gras, which opened in 1954 on Copeland Street. Instead of a cocktail hour, Le Mardi Gras had a "happy hour" from 4:00 p.m. to 7:00 p.m., when martinis two and a half times the size of a regular one were offered for the same price. The bar called this drink a Texas.

Prior to the flower power decade, the bar was a place of coffeehouses and beatniks reading poetry. Le Mardi Gras was where hippies met old-timers, according to a retrospective published in the *Post-Gazette* in 1995. Lou's and the coffeehouse Loaves and Fishes were the places subversive activities were planned. There were after-hour clubs and neighborhood theaters that showed films by Andy Warhol and Frank Zappa.

"I can close my eyes and visualize on any given Friday or Saturday just how crowded and how much music there was," drummer H.B. Bennett told *Post-Gazette* music critic Scott Mervis. "You would get on Walnut and suddenly the cars moved so slow. Everyone was curious. You were looking at them, they were looking at you."

Tension arose because the old-timers resented the longhaired rebels. And the hippies didn't trust anyone over thirty. Everything had a political overtone. Anyone who loitered too long on the street was arrested and thrown into jail. Shadyside was a place of artists, of creative sorts, and that customer base extended into its mixology.

The bartenders in Shadyside took pride in their reputation as expert mixologists. In the early 1960s, three neighborhood bartenders had cards printed with degrees after their names in the early 1960s. Bob Terrick was a Doctor of Mixology. Tony Vinciguerra was a Master of Mixology. Mark Frantz was a Mixologist Supreme.

Frantz came up with a few cocktails, including the Bicentennial cocktail, which was unveiled on Thanksgiving in 1958. The ingredients were maple sugar, vodka and lemon juice. Frantz also developed the Renaissance cocktail, which included bourbon or vodka, honey and fresh grapefruit juice.

"After the first, you feel redeveloped. After the second, you have a 'new look,'" Danver said. "And after the third—you know you're a world leader."

Interest in fancy cocktails began to wane later in the 1960s. In one column written for the *Post-Gazette* in the middle of the 1960s, the writer, Andrew Bernhard, said bartenders no longer needed long repertoires. People were not ordering Pink Ladies, Brandy Alexanders or Old-Fashioneds.

"I note a considerable number of pre-luncheon drinkers ordering a Bloody Mary, and indeed the rise in the consumption of vodka has been one of the main changes in the beverage industry," Bernhard wrote. "But the outstanding development has been the decrease in the demand for complicated drinks such as used to send the bartender to the Bartender's Guide for instructions."

Bartenders would transition into being a friend of customers. They were valued for their counsel rather than their cocktail expertise. At neighborhood corner pubs, they were sometimes closer than brothers or sisters. People went to talk about the Steelers, church, politics and their family problems.

Bartenders, though appreciated less in Pittsburgh for mixology during this time, began to take on an indispensable support role for the community, which was populated with returning veterans traumatized by Vietnam as well as an increasing number of steel millworkers who were losing their jobs. For these groups, therapists were either too expensive or seen as something used by less masculine men.

The veterans' hospitals have historically not been very helpful to people suffering from the invisible wounds of war. Bartenders, in Pittsburgh and around the country, heard problems, offered solutions and insights and helped them overcome their troubles through encouragement. They looked out for them.

Though beer-and-shot bartenders are often disparaged among craft cocktail barkeeps, some who work at VFWs and other places can form a more sincere connection with their patrons or, more accurately, friends they serve. Journalists acknowledged that fact. The *Post-Gazette* published an editorial in 1972 called, "Bartender as Psychiatrist."

"The bartender's psychiatric insight is dearly won," the editorial said. "He must often listen to long stream-of-consciousness monologues more candid than the free-association revelations of analysts during the expensive fifty-dollar hour. The mixologist must placate the belligerent patron with the same painstaking care he lavishes on a Pousse Café."

By 1972, Walnut Street had become unfashionable for young people. Young couples still came there, and the restaurants brought in a lot of business. But the place was no longer a mecca for teenagers and rebellious hippies. It was just too expensive for them to go there. They opted instead for Oakland and the rock clubs that began springing up in the neighborhood closest to the universities. Loaves and Fishes Coffeehouse moved to Oakland. The Encore kept its doors open until May 13, 1982, giving it a twenty-five-year run.

"I'd say friendship is the legacy of that place," Lynn Shiner said. "A lot of friendships were made there. That bar really provided a sense of community for a lot of people. I think that was nice for people in that area."

Seeing all this and taking in the local nightlife was a young man named Tom Jayson. He was somewhat of a barfly, but also an observer of what people wanted from their bars and nightclubs. In his travels throughout the city and country, he would discover the next big trend that he would introduce to Pittsburgh.

And along with the woman he met early on, he would go on to revolutionize the city's nightlife. The next chapter in the city's bar culture was largely a love story between Jayson and his wife.

Beatnik Bender

The Beatnik Bender was created at the Encore Lounge in Shadyside during the 1950s and 1960s. The lounge was a hot spot for jazz musicians and countercultural types. They put their own spin on cocktails.

2 ounces brandy
¾ ounce Benedictine
½ ounce blackberry cordial

This cocktail needs to be stirred. I stick to very strict guidelines for shaking versus stirring cocktails. Stir when all components are alcohol, sugars or bitters; shake when a recipe calls for ingredients that are not alcohol based (i.e.; fruit juices, creams, eggs, et cetera). A martini with gin, vermouth and bitters, composed entirely of alcohol, would be stirred, as would an Old-Fashioned with whiskey, bitters and a sugar cube. In an Old-Fashioned or Sazerac, the sugars are typically soaked with bitters and muddled, creating its own boozy, slurry ingredient. This cocktail, however, I would break the rules on. Knowing the time frame that this cocktail existed in, the creator of this drink intended it to be shaken. Shaking is meant to aerate a cocktail, make it light and give it some zip. Using the double strain method, you can shake your ingredients as hard as you'd like, fully integrating all the flavors and imparting a maximum chill into the cocktail. I would imagine this drink would be better served as a shaken drink for all the hippie kids hanging out in Pittsburgh in the 1960s. Combine all your ingredients in a mixing tin, add ice and shake vigorously. Double strain into a chilled martini glass and garnish with a lemon peel.

5

THE DISCO CLUB ERA

om Jayson saw the lines outside discotheques in Philadelphia and Cleveland early in the 1970s.

When he first tried to attract investors for his own club, they were reticent about giving him the loans. They didn't think discos would go over in Pittsburgh. Eventually, he convinced them that if it worked in a blue-collar rust-belt town like Cleveland, it would work in Pittsburgh. So he established a discotheque on the North Side called 2001. It was an unlikely place to set up shop at the time.

"There was nothing on the North Side," Jayson said at his bar, Homerun Harry's in Station Square. "Across the street, they had a big plant. There weren't any residential places in the immediate area. There was a lot of industrial type of places. It was easy to get to, though. And there was parking. Big clubs like that do well with traffic."

There were some hiccups at first. Jayson bought the biggest speakers he could find. But they weren't commercial speakers, and they started to fail in the first two weeks because they played the music too loud. A sound maintenance man had to extinguish a fire that burst from the speakers. Eventually, the disco made enough money to get high-quality commercial speakers.

The disco was a hit. The lines Jayson saw in Pittsburgh were just as long as the ones in Philadelphia and Cleveland. And that club and others Jayson would own attracted celebrities. Jayson remembers Jack Lambert coming in. Lambert wore all white and leaned against the wall. He never danced. Terry Bradshaw and the other quarterbacks also visited. They came to chase girls.

While working the door one night, he saw a pretty woman leave the club. Jayson asked her why, and she told him she didn't like it there.

Her name was Maggie. She eventually became his wife. She played a big part in the evolution of the disco scene in the city. Maggie was a teacher at Penn Hills High School before she met Tom Jayson. She eventually quit her job to help Tom Jayson develop a nightclub in Ohio. From then on, she would play an important role in developing his nightclub empire.

Maggie Jayson was attracted to Tom's ambition and imagination.

"He had a vision. Of anyone I knew here, he had one," she said over coffee. "All of his friends would tell him it would never work. I think entrepreneurs, we take chances."

Jayson had an intriguing backstory. His experiences and travels enabled him to bounce back from adversity. Jayson grew up on the South Side. His father never made more than $125 a week. He was a pinsetter at Pine Valley Lanes on Route 88 when he was in grade school. His schooling ended at the eighth grade at the age of fifteen.

He sold baby pictures for New Deal Studios on the South Side, making $200 to $300 a week. He was in magazine sales and handwriting analysis in the 1960s. Jayson moved all over the Eastern Seaboard before coming back to Pittsburgh.

A year after opening 2001, he was bought out for $12,000 following a dispute about management. But it was not the end of his nightclub reign.

He began franchising his ability to design and package discos. He called his company 2001 Clubs of America and advertised it on an NBC show in 1976. The producers of the show got about three thousand calls the next day of people interested in the club. When he got some franchises sold, he opened the VIP Club in Bridgeville in 1976.

Pittsburgher James Kowalczyk, who was an investor in his nightclub operation, explained Jayson's strengths to the *Post-Gazette* in 1989. "He has a good reading on the public," Kowalczyk said. "He understands people and the ordinary guy. That's because he's streetwise. He made it on his own, without family money or help. When he designs his club, he uses himself as a guide. Judging by his track record, if he likes it, chances are the public will too."

Discotheques became the fashionable places to party in Pittsburgh during the 1970s into the early 1980s. The disco craze hit Pittsburgh in late 1974. Disc jockeys were cheaper than bands, and so bar owners preferred to hire them to supply the music. A wave of dances came in with the discos— the hustle, the basketball, muscle, body language, bus stop and Spiderman.

The August 17, 1976 edition of the *Post-Gazette* told of the disco craze that took hold of the city. *Copyright © Pittsburgh Post-Gazette, 2016, all rights reserved. Reprinted with permission.*

In Pittsburgh, there were ten discos in 1976, but five more would soon open up. The dancers didn't like the Acid Rock scene.

"We used to carry our stack of old 45s (mostly soul dancing records from the Motown era) and go to all these parties, but we felt kind of weird because nobody else was dancing. So when discos became popular, we were ready," twenty-three-year-old Celeste Begandy told the *Post-Gazette*.

At the Backstage in the Holiday House, blue jeans were prohibited. Spaghetti-strapped gowns of chiffon and lace were quite common. The men wore three-piece European-cut suits. The kids weren't as into politics as their '60s counterparts were. They just wanted to have fun.

Lines would populate Bouqet Street as people wanted to get into Zelda's Greenhouse in Oakland. Back in 1971, disco music appeared at Oakland's Wooden Keg on Forbes Avenue, the disco craze's granddaddy.

The owner hired disc jockey Porky Chedwick of golden oldies fame to spin records in his cellar.

Chedwick and other deejays like Mad Mike had been spinning record hops daily at lodges, roller rinks, schools, parks and religious institutions throughout the 1960s. Their importance would only increase in the 1970s. By 1978, discos were responsible for an estimated $6 million in liquor sales annually. One owner told the *Post-Gazette* that discos were the "greatest spur to the liquor business since Repeal."

Three of the biggest discos—the Holiday House's Backstage and the two VIP clubs—grossed about $1 million each. The music was prerecorded, which enabled the owners to save money by using deejays instead of bands, which cost more.

Deejays earned about $50 to $100 a night. A deejay at one of the bigger clubs could earn about $25,000 to $30,000 a year.

"The disc jockey is very important," said Bert Sokol, owner of the Backstage. "He must be able to program the music to the kind of people we attract. If he didn't have the ability to do this judiciously, we would have problems. People simply would be turned off and go somewhere else."

Special disco parties and dance contests were important promotions. Discos were fashionable among all crowds. Since discos were so popular with women, they also became a popular place for men to go. Shelley Smilack, a disco dancer, told the *Post-Gazette* bad television shows got people out of the house. Discotheques were also popular among married couples.

"I'm glad it's taking off," Smilack said. "It has sociological overtones that are healthy. People are doing things together. What a relief after that hassle in the 1960s when everybody hated everybody else and psychedelic music was in and the world was in a mess. It's great to see people out there enjoying themselves."

Different discos attracted different crowds, according to the *Post-Gazette*. The Backstage drew the fashionable, boutique-set who were interested in clothing styles as much as they were dancing.

The Library in the Bank, in downtown, attracted junior executives in three-piece suits and their secretaries looking for a man. The Next Step in the Marriott drew hip suburban crowds. Zelda's drew the college crowd. And the Giraffe, in Parkway Center, seemed to attract young singles.

Drinks were not overpriced, and there was seldom a cover charge. Median price for a mixed drink was $1.50.

The discos took off in the suburbs as well. Every Sunday night, the Trolley Bar Lounge of the Marriott in Green Tree would turn into a disco. It was started as an oldies night, with Porky Chedwick behind the turntables at first. People would be ten-deep at the bar. They played radio-oriented dance hits rather than hardcore disco tunes heard in regular discos. Many of the Pittsburgh Steelers showed up on Sunday nights. They went on until 1:30 a.m.

In 1979, eleven thousand people applied for disco lessons in special classes offered by the Community College of Allegheny County, according to a *Post-Gazette* article.

At 2001 and the VIP clubs that eventually developed, Jayson and his wife were innovative in setting the ambience. Maggie did the lighting and most of the multimedia.

Maggie was a photographer, and she would travel to the cities where they had started a club to get panoramic pictures of the community. The photos she took would then be used in a multimedia show that would kick off the dancing.

"It was mesmerizing. It was the whole flavor of disco with all the visuals. It was awesome," she said. "It was like going to Disney World."

All their shows started with David Bowie's "Space Oddity" in the background. Sixty seconds after the first sound, it would go into total darkness, and on the screen you would see a countdown. The pictures Maggie took would be used on large screens before the dancing got underway.

"Everyone would stand on their chairs," Tom Jayson said in an interview. "It was something to see. The whole show lasted twenty to thirty minutes. Then it would go to dancing."

In Pittsburgh, they built four VIP clubs. And they took over Heaven, which they bought from Rick Stern in the 1980s.

"It was downtown. It was a beautiful club," Jayson said. "Stern called me and said he would be closing it and asked if I would be interested in buying it. That was probably the most unique club built in Pittsburgh."

The club was renamed Mirage. It received a half-million-dollar renovation, according to the *Post-Gazette*. Mirage had pressed-marble terrazzo on the first floor. Seven bars were located throughout the club. Five large screens played music videos. One screen was the largest in the country at two hundred square feet, according to Jayson.

The club had flash dancers who were on raised platforms at the center of the club. If you wanted a little privacy, there were mini-suites you could book to take a guest to while you drank champagne. People of varying backgrounds used those suites. There was special treatment for certain people.

"Back then, they had a book of the most eligible bachelors," Jayson said "And if you wanted to, you could rent a room. If they were there, they got the room for free. And if you wanted, you could get a key and a bottle for twenty-five dollars."

An eighteen-year-old would-be carpenter named Jimmy King got his first bartending gig at Mirage. He worked the area where the champagne rooms were.

"I was given keys to the cubby holes," King said, reflecting on his early days. "You'd get champagne and the room for the night. The first five were prostitutes. The next seven were drug dealers. And the rest were regular people."

The bartending gigs at the mega clubs were lucrative. When King went home to show his father how much money he had made in his first week, his father took a look at the big wad of money his son had and told him that he was going to be a bartender for the rest of his life.

King would grow close to Tom Jayson, eventually becoming one of his closest advisors, Maggie Jayson said.

"I guess some of these people felt they were in a cult," Maggie said. "When you talk to Jimmy King, it amazes me when he talks about how much time he says he spent with Tom [Jayson]. I thought people got so entwined in the nightclub. I think it's because of the glamour. You could really get wrapped up in it."

Though disco reigned in the 1970s and early 1980s, other scenes developed throughout the city. Downtown earned a reputation in the 1970s as a nice place to go for people with money. Around 9:00 p.m., car and pedestrian traffic swelled along Grant Street, Liberty Avenue and Market Square.

"I've gotta put out 50 bucks for two guys on Fridays to keep people out," said Buddie Stevenson, of Buddies on Market Street, to the *Post-Gazette*. "And that's after we've doubled capacity by taking out half the tables."

Friday and Wednesday nights were the biggest ones in the week for the downtown area. By some estimates, five thousand people poured into the Golden Triangle on Friday nights. The opening of Three Rivers Stadium and Heinz Hall helped. Civic Arena concerts also brought people into the city. Police patrols and the feeling of safety also made the area an attractive one to party.

Will Shiner opened another Encore club downtown. Top Shelf on Liberty Avenue also brought in crowds. Generally, it was a suit-and-tie crowd.

Drinks could be pricey for the time downtown. Highballs, martinis and Manhattans sold for $1.25. Beer was usually $0.75 or $1.00 per bottle. Exotic mixtures like Singapore Slings and Harvey Wallbangers were more expensive, according to a 1973 *Post-Gazette* article.

Mixed drinks were regaining popularity in the 1970s. Robert Paganico, the Pittsburgh Bartenders' Institute's chief instructor, knew five hundred drinks by memory. The *Post-Gazette* compared him to a pharmacology professor.

Paganico worked at Bob's Garage in Fox Chapel. He said the key to being a good bartender and making a good drink was knowing how the customer liked his drinks. Secret ingredients and special shakes made no difference, he said.

"Every good bartender knows he's supposed to listen and not repeat—this business is like being a lawyer, priest, psychologist and a doctor to your customers," Paganico told his students.

The Moscow Mule may not have been Pittsburgh's favorite drink at the better bars, but it was ordered enough to be included in the standard list of drinks the Pittsburgh Bartender Institute made its students memorize.

Before opening, the institute hired a consultant to find out what Pittsburghers were drinking. From that, the basic list was made. They revised it once a year as fad drinks came and went.

The Godfather became a popular drink when the movies came out. So did the Godmother.

The list included familiar drinks like the martini but also lesser-known drinks like the Piña Colada, Ramos Gin Fizz and the Salty Dog. And there were also revived drinks like the Zombie.

Jazz, rock music, pop hits, the Steelers and the Pirates all attracted people to downtown. Adult theaters also got people to visit the area. The shot-and-beer crowd went to the Oyster House and Benny's New Diamond Café in Market Square.

Another nightclub downtown that made waves in the 1980s and 1990s was Pegasus, which was a gay bar. It was known as a twink-and-drag bar. (Twinks were thin young men, while drags were the men they pursued.)

The actress Kathleen Turner visited the club when she came to star in a local production.

"Everybody tried to out dress everybody," Richard Vinski, a patron of the club, told the *Post-Gazette*'s Marylynne Pitz years later. "We used to dance with our shirts off and, of course, the straight women loved us."

Gay people had a circuit in downtown Pittsburgh in the 1980s. They would go to Venture Inn for cocktails, stop at Cruella De Ville, where men danced in bird cages, and then move on to Zack's Fourth Avenue, a dance club, before ending up for fancy cocktails at Pegasus.

In Oakland, a music scene began to take shape in the 1970s. Dom DiSilvio opened the Decade in 1973. He booked mostly local oldies bands at the club

Dominic "Dom" DiSilvio, promoter, stands in front of the Decade in Oakland in the fall of 1993. *Photo by Bill Wade; copyright © Pittsburgh Post-Gazette, 2016, all rights reserved. Reprinted with permission.*

at first. It became one of the hippest music clubs in the area, with national acts coming through, including the Ramones, the Police and U2.

"This was in the true sense a showcase club," DiSilvio would later tell *City Paper*. "You could showcase a group and the audience could intermingle with the group when a break came. They might sign autographs, touch them, talk to them, get laid up in the office, whatever. And that's what sells records. It's a grassroots thing and that can only happen in a club like the Decade."

Graffiti was another club that showcased bands. It had pricier drinks than the Decade and the Banana. It was bigger and harder to fill than the latter two. But it found its niche by catering to the MTV crowd. The Clarks were a popular band that played in the club.

The Electric Banana was a popular venue in Oakland. John Zarra, later known as Johnny Banana, was the owner of the club. He had pioneered go-go dancing in the city when he opened the Spotlite. Eventually, some of the biggest acts in the world would come through, including the Red Hot Chili Peppers and Meat Loaf. U2 almost came through, but by that time, they wanted too much money.

The Banana was originally a black disco from 1977 to 1979. But as disco faded, it became a scene for punk and new wave youths.

"The Banana got to be the Banana because no one would book new wave or punk," Zarra said in an interview. "They were all nice educated kids. They were CMU students, Pitt students."

The Banana also had some interesting cocktails created by Judy Zarra, known for her brusqueness. She had one called the Rude Judy, which consisted of amaretto, blue curaçao and Daily's Cocktail Mix.

"We had the Rude Judy," Judy Zarra said. "One of the bands gave it to me. I gave it to him and it was blue. And he said you should call it the rude Judy."

An exterior shot of the Electric Banana, a popular club in Oakland in the 1980s and 1990s. *Photo courtesy Stephen R. Bodner.*

Judy and Johnny Zarra outside the Electric Banana on New Year's Eve 1986. *Photo by Andy Starnes; copyright* © Pittsburgh Post-Gazette, *2016, all rights reserved. Reprinted with permission.*

The Banana was not part of a barhopping scene like today's South Side.

"This place had to be a destination," John Zarra said. "It was 'where are you going tonight?' And it was, 'I'm going to the Banana.' You have to be better than all the rest of them for people to come here."

Dewey Gurall was a longtime frequenter of the Decade and other clubs in Oakland. In the 1970s, he wrote for *Pittsburgh Music* magazine, which held editorial meetings at the Decade. For him and others plugged into the Oakland scene, there was a sense that they didn't fit in with what the rest of the city was doing.

"We definitely had an 'us and them' mentality with the disco people in the late '70s and '80s," Gurall said over the phone. "The people who were into the Iron City Houserockers, we wouldn't have been caught dead in a disco."

The Oakland scene people were musical purists. Gurall said:

> *I think if you were a music person, you didn't want to go dance. That was something guys did to go find girls. If you wanted to see a band, you didn't want to see them play hits on the radio. Music people gravitated to these types of clubs. It tended to be alternative people. The more career-oriented people, who dressed up nice on the weekend didn't go to the Banana or the Decade. They stayed away from those places.*

Mount Lebanon was another area that began attracting crowds in the 1970s. In 1975, voters in that town ended the dry policy that had been around for thirty-six years. Bars such as the Saloon and the Sunken Cork became popular places for singles to go.

"They used to roll the sidewalks up here at 9 p.m.," recalled Wayne Pritchard, co-owner of the Sunken Cork, to the *Post-Gazette*. "People who worked here went to Dormont for a drink, and people who lived here stayed downtown for happy hour."

The two locations became the fastest growing in town. The Saloon was a shot-and-a-beer place. It remains open today. Owner Jim Sheppard hoped it would grow into the vibrant place for youth.

"What we'd like to see happen is to see it turn into a Shadyside," Sheppard said to the *Post-Gazette* in the 1970s.

The Saloon attracted some of the more prominent athletes in town, including many of the Steelers and Penguins.

"We'd get a lot of linemen," Sheppard told *Mt. Lebanon Magazine*. "They'd come in on Monday or Tuesday when they were off to unwind. We'd get a lot of hockey players. They were all personable. They'd come in for lunch hour because we used to be open for it then."

The seeds for the South Side's renaissance were planted in the 1980s. The South Side, as it's seen today, is an eclectic mix of bars, coffee shops, beauty salons and other storefronts. But it wasn't that way thirty-five years ago.

When you drove through the neighborhood, there were boarded buildings and a few bars, including Jack's, Dee's Café and Kotula's. But that began to change when Bob Pessolano opened Mario's in the early 1980s.

"This changed the perception of the South Side," Bob's son Louis Pessolano said while sitting in the Mario's as it currently stands. "Jack's has changed their way of doing things. Dee's has as well. But those weren't bars that attracted kids from Duquesne, Pitt and young professionals. They attracted steel mill workers. And the mills were leaving at that point."

Those familiar with the neighborhood were surprised that someone would open a bar catering to the yuppie and college crowd in such a downtrodden neighborhood. But the bar became a hit.

Bob Pessolano was always trying to find an avenue that would interest people just by seeing it. He had a number of drinks where he would put

The first Mario's on the South Side was the catalyst for two decades of economic growth in the neighborhood. *Photo by Bill Campbell; copyright © Pittsburgh Post-Gazette, 2016, all rights reserved. Reprinted with permission.*

beer in different vessels just so people would see the fancy drinks, which would make it more likely for them to buy them. They had yards and port-a-potty glasses. They had fishbowl drinks. Anything that he could find in trade magazines, Pessolano was willing to try.

The bar faced a number of nuisance complaints over loud noise and public urination from customers streaming out of the bar.

"Like everything, not everyone is going to see it as they want it," Louis Pessolano said. "They want one establishment or that establishment to be responsible for everyone who comes down here. And that's not going to work out that way."

However, there was also a large contingent of people in the area who were happy money was coming back into the neighborhood after an economic depression.

Bob Pessolano's success enabled him to purchase the building next door, where he expanded Mario's into Lula's.

There wasn't a huge beer selection at Mario's. Pessolano had maybe five, his son said. They didn't make crazy cocktails either. But Mario's was always on the cutting edge.

"My dad and his family went to the distributor of Corona in Chicago," Louis Pessolano said. "And he was the first bar to have Corona bottles. And it went over like gangbusters. My dad saw what people were doing elsewhere, and tried to get it here first."

Mario's was more of a sports bar that was an appealing option for college kids to come to on the weekend. Within a few years of Mario's opening, more bars came to town. Investors saw the South Side as an up-and-coming neighborhood.

It also laid the foundation for what would be the epicenter of the cocktail revolution that would begin in the 1990s.

Station Square began to attract business in the 1980s, most notably Chauncy's, which was owned by Jayson. It opened in 1983 and had a twenty-year run.

"Back then, Station Square was just getting started," Jayson said. "They had the Grand Concourse. They had Houlihan's. It was by the hotel.

"Chauncy's was upscale. We sold food. The dining area was good. We had a guy at the door who wore a tuxedo. It wasn't a kids place. It was for Yuppies."

Chauncy's was well reviewed by Mike Kalina for the *Post-Gazette*.

"Chauncy's is one of only a few dining/dancing spots in the district," Kalina wrote. "But we may be seeing more of them in years to come.

Chauncy's at Station Square was known as one of the best places to meet singles in the city when it was open. *Photo by Joyce Mendelsohn; copyright © Pittsburgh Post-Gazette, 2016, all rights reserved. Reprinted with permission.*

Maturing disco habitués may want more than just drinks, flashing lights and a dance floor when they decide to spend a night out under one roof."

Jimmy King bartended at the club for years. The club's appeal was simple to him.

"If you couldn't get laid in Chauncy's, you may as well have joined the priesthood, and vice versa," King said.

Since there was such a wide age range of people who came in, they served more than one thousand drinks.

"You couldn't just come off the streets and be a bartender," King said. "You had to be barback for two years before being considered a bartender at Chauncy's."

Nightclubs would continue to dominate the area over the next few decades. They would stay true to the formula established by Jayson.

"I've been 30 years in the business," King said. "The wheel has never been reinvented. Only the names and faces change. It's the same wheel going around and around."

The dance floor at Chauncy's was one of the most hopping in the city. It attracted people from all backgrounds. *Photo by Bob Donaldson; copyright* © Pittsburgh Post-Gazette, *2016, all rights reserved. Reprinted with permission.*

O'Halloran's Blarney Buster

Lenny O'Halloran, T.G.I.F. Monroeville

This cocktail was the first-place winner of the Jameson Irish Cocktail Contest held in Monroeville in March 1983, Jameson's first event in the Pittsburgh market.

1 ½ ounces Jameson Irish Whiskey
½ ounce Bailey's Irish Cream
½ ounce Kahlua
½ ounce Grand Marnier
Fill: coffee

Always heat a hot drink mug before pouring your drink in, just as you should always chill your cold cocktail glasses. Pour scalding hot water into the mug to prep the glass. Pour this hot water out before you make the drink. This drink technique is what is called a "build," where all the ingredients are poured directly into the serving glass instead of being prepared, stirred or shaken in a separate vessel. In this instance, we will combine ingredients in heated mug. Give a quick stir to integrate flavors and add black coffee to fill. Top with whipped cream and color with a little bit of green crème de menthe.

6

THE NIGHTCLUB SHUFFLE

On Metropol's opening day, hundreds of people arrived in a variety of fashions, including leather jackets, chiffon and Bermuda shorts with a tux jacket. The first person they saw upon entering was Paul Hauber, a Duquesne senior who was wearing a black tux with coordinated tie, cummerbund and a pocket handkerchief. He had jelled his long hair to stand straight up. A truck ramp stood at the entrance, and antiques were in the washroom. The exterior had hundreds of glass windows, covered in grime, surrounded by weathered red bricks. The dance floor seemed like a loading dock. The lighting included floor strobes, workmen's lanterns and diamond-plate pylons. Multilevel catwalks, fences and fresh beams filled the club. Wiring conduits and heating ducts were not hidden. The club combined the industrial feel of the city with the MTV sensibilities embodied by the 1980s generation.

"As Pittsburgh comes out of the industrial age and becomes a cultural city, I thought of blending the two, of marrying those elements, and offering an alternate form of entertainment for all ages," Robin Fernandez told the *Post-Gazette* in 1988 when it opened. Fernandez, at the time a thirty-year-old who prior to Metropol had run a club in Green Tree called Confetti, operated it. He, his brother Eric and restaurateur Damian Soffer were the owners.

Fernandez grew up in Donora and studied food administration at Indiana University of Pennsylvania. As would become apparent to a generation of Pittsburghers, Fernandez was willing to try something different, even if it seemed destined to fail. Fernandez believed the Strip

District was a viable neighborhood to open a club, despite people who urged him to locate it elsewhere.

The Pittsburgh Zoning Board of Adjustment tried to convince him it was a bad idea to put a club in the Strip District. They told him it had no chance of succeeding as a club. The board gave him the approval despite expectations it would fail.

"I said we should open up in the Strip District in a warehouse, but they thought I was crazy," he said while sitting at his current club in Sewickley. "I started doing more research and developing an idea and a concept. I established a relationship with the owner of the building. And I decided to pull the trigger."

Fernandez's faith was well rewarded. The club became a success. The eclectic mixture of cultures that visited it made it the most fashionable and vibrant nightclub in Pittsburgh. Straight and gay people came in, rich and poor, black and white, alternative and yuppie. It was a break from the discotheque.

"I think what we created and developed in the '80s was the forefront of all this happening," Fernandez said. "Everything was middle of the road. They were coming out of the disco era. Then it died, and there were all these social meeting places that cropped up that were like mini-clubs."

Mario Lemieux hailed the club as the most fashionable in the city to out-of-town publications. Lou Reed came there, though he refused to perform for an audience that expected him to. Chanel held a launch party at Metropol. From there, the Strip District became an attractive neighborhood to locate a business.

"People saw the opportunity in the Strip," Fernandez said. "The produce business was starting to fade and spaces were becoming available. Parking was free. So it was natural for the club, bar and restaurant business to meld right into that."

Tom Jayson saw what was happening. After establishing Chauncy's, which had been the most popular nightclub in town, he eyed the Strip District as the next great neighborhood. He tried to raise $50 million to build a waterfront entertainment complex in the Strip District that he told *Post-Gazette* writer Mike Kalina in 1989 would be the culmination of his career. The project was called "The Strip—Down by the Riverside."

"It will be the largest sports nightclub and restaurant complex in the world," Jayson told Kalina. "Here as you enter, will be moving mannequins of Steelers and Pirates in costume. The kids will love it. There will also be souvenir concessions, ticket outlets and a board showing the Vegas odds on various sports."

Tom Jayson and Elaine Hall show the plans he had for the Strip District Waterfront Complex. *Photo by Bill Levis; copyright* © Pittsburgh Post-Gazette, *2016, all rights reserved. Reprinted with permission.*

Jayson wanted to establish a marina, an entertainment complex and a nightclub that could accommodate 1,500 for dancing and 3,500 for concerts. He wanted to put in a comedy club, too.

Those plans never came to fruition. But Jayson eventually opened Donzi's and Tequila Willies on the Boardwalk. He found the clubs did well seasonally.

"[Tequila Willies] was on the water. Boats could come up in the Strip," Jayson said during an interview. "There was a place in Florida where boats could come and people could party. But the problem with that location is the wintertime. It's ten degrees. They're not going to walk across the bridge that's icy to get there. And the only view was the ice in the river. We didn't draw anybody then. We did well from Memorial Day to Labor Day."

Jimmy King went to bartend at Donzi's when it opened in 1992.

"It was crazy," King said in an interview. "On the whole boardwalk, the only thing that was open was Donzi's. All the others weren't open. It was the best money I ever made in my life. Every bartender down there bought new cars within two months. We were making so much money. Then September first hit, and the cold front hit, and the city of Pittsburgh shut down. They weren't expecting that. We all had car payments that winter we couldn't handle."

Fernandez began to expand his business. He also opened Rosebud, a jazz venue, in the Strip. Fernandez has a lot of war stories from his time as a nightclub owner, including one that happened at Rosebud.

"I remember one night, David Crosby came and played," Fernandez said. "After shows, Rosebud would turn into a dance club. Both places would turn into a club. After he was done playing, he was socializing and the programmer put on dance music, but he got upset we were playing certain music. So we got in a heated exchange. I told him his show was over, and we were setting up for the evening. He didn't like that."

The South Side was becoming a destination neighborhood at the same time that the Strip was growing.

Bob Pessolano opened Nick's Fat City in July 1992. Like Mario's, it was met by locals with criticism of loud noise and public disturbances. The black-and-white floor was inlaid with three-foot stars enshrining notables like Stephen Foster, George Benson, Larry Lee Jones, Shirley Jones and Lena Horne. In total, it memorialized fifty-eight stars of the local Pittsburgh music scene. Pessolano opened Nick's Fat City because he wanted to create a niche market for local performers, his son Louis said.

"They felt that Pittsburgh lacked a quality venue to see local bands, but could house smaller national bands to come in," Louis Pessolano said. "They had various types of music."

The music club had memorabilia lining the walls. Rows of autographed guitars adorned the place, as did other instruments owned by famous musicians. A pair of snakeskin boots autographed by Stevie Ray Vaughan was on display. So was a Jethro Tull flute. A star even memorialized the Decade, which Pessolano said was necessary because the place was an institution.

The upstairs bar had nine television sets. Nick's occupancy was six hundred people, though it struggled at first to get people to come in. Mostly that was due to the barrier preventing music crowds from getting alcohol. It took a long time for Pessolano to get a liquor license extended to that part of the facility.

"It was the worst situation you could ever imagine," Bob Pessolano told the *Post-Gazette* a few months after it opened.

Nick's Fat City became the go-to place for rockers. It featured Hootie & the Blowfish, the Strokes and three appearances by Bruce Springsteen, who was playing with Joe Grushecky.

By 1995, the South Side had undergone a remarkable transformation in the bar crowds it attracted. Before Mario's opened, Jack's had been a bar where working men, unemployed men and old retired guys went, according to an *In Pittsburgh Newsweekly* article.

It still had that feel during the day. But by the mid-'90s, Jack's had at night become a bar where twenty-somethings mingled. Women rarely went into the bar before, but in the '90s, college-aged women wearing dresses and donning perfume went there to play pool. On the weekends, it looked like a fraternity party.

"South Side used to look like a lot of old guys consoling themselves at a bar and watching the traffic go by," *In Pittsburgh* writer Brian Connelly said. "Now it looks like a 23-year-old suburban guy pulling up in a new Chevy Lumina blasting Rusted Root out of the window."

While the South Side was booming, the Oakland scene was beginning to decline. Some people attributed it to rent becoming too high, but others said it was because the University of Pittsburgh wanted to curtail its reputation as a party school. Whatever it was, people went elsewhere for live music as the twenty-first century approached.

"The thing about the South Side, it was interesting with its rise. It's kind of a law of physics thing," Gurall said. "As Oakland deflated, the South Side rose."

Some, including Gurall, think it was the beginning of the decline of Pittsburgh's vibrant music scene: "The South Side became the place to go, which was fine. But now you had a situation where it was so congested, and there was no longer…everyone went everywhere. It was a nightmare to park on the weekends. A lot of people my age were starting to say, 'Oh hell, it's not worth it.' I think that killed a lot of music and local music."

John Zarra thought it was a generational problem. "The problem, the main problem is they don't support the bands or the clubs like they did back in the day," he said. "And the club owners can't stay in business unless they go to see them."

Joe Grushecky and the Houserockers played the last show at the Decade on August 21, 1995. It remained open for a few years as the Next Decade before closing permanently. On January 15, 2000, the last band to ever play at the Electric Banana performed. A few months later, it was announced Graffiti would close its doors.

"The vital signs don't look good; the prognosis is grim," Mary Binder wrote for *City Paper* that year. "The local music scene's health seems questionable with the announcement of Graffiti's closing."

At Station Square, a number of clubs would come and go throughout the nightclub era. Matrix, Margarita Mamas, Saddle Ridge and Bar Room

Pittsburgh were a few that were located in the East Warehouse, which was a destination spot for clubbers into the mid-2000s. And Chauncy's was still in the freight station. But they all fell on hard times, and the wave of club shootings in the city specifically hit the Strip District and Station Square. The district attorney and other public officials targeted those places to close.

Station Square would suffer from competition from the Waterfront, which featured a variety of fashionable restaurants, a Dave and Busters and the Improv, which became a popular comedy club. Bar Louie on the Waterfront was a popular venue.

Jayson sold Chauncy's in the early 2000s. After the transition, the new owners were caught in a heroin ring that led to its closure. The East Warehouse was knocked down in 2014 to make room for residential complexes.

Nightclubs currently in the city have fallen to two or three successful ones, including Cavo and Diesel.

"Back in my day before these clubs, it was always an understanding you needed Friday and Saturday and one other night to have a successful club," King said. "Nightclubs are a thing of the past where you can go there every night.

Jayson's Strip District club empire also was hit by the crime wave, including Tequila Willies.

"Ownership didn't want the dealing with the killings and shootings," King said. "That played a big part in closing down Station Square. It was because there were organized gangs. They're targeted because that's where all the shootings are."

In addition to Station Square, the Strip was declining due to crime. Fernandez said, "The Strip got very violent. The shootings, the knifings and the fighting. All those things started to do a lot of damage. The Strip had its downfall and the South Side had its resurrection. There was a battle of publicity between South Side bars and the Strip clubs and bars. We'd find flyers all over our customers' cars that said people should come over the South Side and stay away from the violent Strip."

Jayson disagreed that it became too violent: "There were a couple clubs where there were bad elements. But I don't think it was that bad. Shootings happen everywhere. When it happens in the nightclub, they go nuts. Prior to the '90s, people didn't have guns. They had knives. You didn't hear much about shootings until the '90s. If I'm in a bar, if there was a guy over there with a knife, I was safe. If a guy has a gun, and he starts shooting, I can't escape."

For Jayson, his legacy of being the most influential Pittsburgh nightclub owner of his generation remains intact. But he realizes that what he did future entrepreneurs will not repeat. While music blared at his bar, Jayson said:

> *There's a professor at Stanford University. And he was on a TV station talking about how the news media has evolved from being news into being entertainment. He said that all entertainment goes out of style. And I thought, "Man, you hit the nail on the head."*
>
> *How long does a hit record stay? How about a Broadway show? How about a TV show? They all go out of style. All entertainment goes out of style. And nightclubs are certainly entertainment.*

Rude Judy

Judy Zarra, Electric Banana

Judy Zarra at the Electric Banana developed this drink during that music club's heyday. It was named after a customer told her that the drink was, "Rude, Judy."

1 ounce amaretto
½ ounce blue curaçao
½ ounce lemon juice
¼ ounce simple syrup
Fill: ginger ale

Combine ingredients, except for ginger ale, in mixing tin with ice and shake. Strain drink over ice in a Collins glass. Double straining is not necessary when pouring from shaker over ice, unless you are pouring over a rocks drink with one cube, or there is an abundance of muddled fruit particles you want to keep from entering the cocktail. When there's multiple cubes in the receiving glass the presence of ice shards and fruit pulp will hardly be noticeable. Fill with ginger ale and add a lemon wedge garnish.

7

COCKTAIL RESURGENCE

The Lava Lounge was different from what people were used to in Pittsburgh. The décor was modern, with bar stools that rolled on tracks. The owners wanted the customers to be uncomfortable enough so they would be inclined to move around the room.

The place would fill nightly with artists, grad students and young professionals. They tested mixed drinks and martinis while listening to both techno and Frank Sinatra. It was the beginning of a new era in the city's nightlife.

"The cocktail revolution cometh," *Post-Gazette* writer Tony Norman wrote in 1996. "It may have been late getting here compared to other cities, but it's here."

Cocktail lounges had become a trend nationwide, and Pittsburgh caught on after the big cities. The neighborhood at the center of it all was the South Side. It started with coffee shops like the Beehive, which was owned by Scott Kramer and Steve Zumoff, the same people who opened Lava Lounge. The coffee shop craze that took hold of the 1990s youth generation established the foundation for people's socializing habits. Lounging and conversation became the preferred way of interacting with friends. The South Side was a place where longtime residents mingled with hipsters, punks and creative types. It was the perfect environment for the cocktail revolution to begin since there was an air of conflict. *City Paper* writer Rich Lord in 1996 wrote:

Sterile is one thing the South Side is not. Shadyside and Squirrel Hill often come off as tony, the Cultural District attracts the turtleneck set, and Smallman Street might as well be called the Strip District U.

But East Carson Street on a good night is a screaming laceration on the city's aging epidermis. If new development kills the spirit which draws together priests, pagans, Pentecostals, curmudgeons, entrepreneurs, politicians, hot dog merchants and the occasional vampire, Pittsburgh will lose something no amount of planning can replace.

But if the diversity which makes the South Side tick can be expanded, if that energy can be tapped, this old town may step a little livelier for the effort.

The South Side earned praise from the *Post-Gazette* as being the most vibrant and eclectic neighborhood in the city. When Mario's opened, the vacancy rate of storefronts was 60 percent. In 2002, it was 7 percent. During that span, 125 faces were restored, 150 new business moved in and six hundred new jobs were created. It wasn't all bars either. There were tattoo parlors, antique shops, art galleries and music venues.

"I think we're the one place in Pittsburgh that borders on being Bohemian," said Carey Harris, executive director of the South Side Local Development Company, to the *Post-Gazette*. "There are other cool neighborhoods, but I think we might have that niche."

Bob Pessolano told the newspaper that he would never have anticipated all that sprang from his bar. "I wish I could say I was smart enough to realize all this would happen, but I really wasn't," Pessolano said. "Not in my wildest dreams. All I wanted to do was survive."

Shot-and-a-beer taverns still endured throughout the South Side and the city, but intimate bars with innovative cocktails began springing up soon after Lava Lounge.

"The community's artistic leanings make for an audience open to previously unexpected possibilities," wrote *In Pittsburgh* writer Lissa Brennan in 1998. "And many of the newer hot spots boast proprietors not too different from their clientele—the young and adventurous not only frequent bars, but own them too."

Lava Lounge hosted theatrical and musical performances. Much in the spirit of the Hill District jazz bars during that neighborhood's golden era, the creativity of the artists filtered down to the bartenders, who came up with interesting cocktails.

Along with the Lava Lounge on the South Side, the Vertigo Bar in Shadyside also pushed the envelope with cocktails. Mad Mex, part of a chain of restaurants that would grow to include Kaya, Casbah and Soba, would also make innovative drinks that would cultivate cocktail tastes in the city.

Club Havana in Shadyside was another interesting cocktail bar. The drink menu there was larger than the food menu. The bar used only fresh ingredients. Banana daiquiris, mojitos and alternative martinis such as mosquitos (vodka, sake and a slice of cucumber) and El Coraje (tequila, a dash of Tabasco and a diced jalapeño) were among the drinks sold at Club Havana.

A batch of talented bartenders would push the city to the fore of the national trend within twenty years. A culture of excellence would start and build within that time, and the way people drank in Pittsburgh would be dramatically different after those two decades passed.

At Lava Lounge, Don Bistarkey was the man behind the revolution. He was named *In Pittsburgh*'s "Bartender of the Year" twice. He could make classic cocktails and provide their historical backstories.

He had a heavy influence on other bartenders in the area, including Sean Enright, who would go on to become a statesman in the local craft cocktail scene.

"Don took the guests' experience to a whole new level," Enright said. "Lava Lounge was a temple to the cocktail while Don was behind the bar. People came to see Don and if he was working that night, chances were you were going to bypass your standard Guinness for an opportunity to have Don make you something you'd never order for yourself…because you'd never heard of it."

Bistarkey, Enright and others would instill a respect for research among younger bartenders. They would pass along book recommendations and other tips for where to learn the craft. There was a drive to master what was already out there. It was about getting the fundamentals right before moving on to experimental bartending.

Enright would soon become the go-to guy for cocktails in the city. Enright, of Norwell, Massachusetts, began his bartending career in Pittsburgh in 2000. He had artistic notions but had not found an outlet for it until he became a bartender.

"I've always had the artist mentality but without having any talent whatsoever for most traditional arts," he told *Pittsburgh Magazine*'s Hal Klein in 2015. "Craft-cocktail bartending is a perfect fit for me."

He would be part of Big Burrito Restaurant Group's craft cocktail revolution when he worked at its Casbah restaurant. At Soba, Enright tinkered with bacon fat–washed whiskey recipes. He would eventually move

The famous Fussfungle cocktail, which took the nation by storm in latter part of the nineteenth and early part of the twentieth centuries. *Photo by Adam Milliron.*

Pittsburghesque cocktail. The drink was named after a famous column that ran in the *Post-Gazette* beginning in the 1920s. *Photo by Adam Milliron.*

London Calling, a cocktail created by Rob
Ricci. *Photo by Adam Milliron.*

The Morning Glory Feast, which
was William Penn bartender George
Kokinakas's favorite morning hangover
cure. *Photo by Adam Milliron.*

The Beatnik Bender, which originated from the Encore Lounge in Shadyside in the late 1950s. *Photo by Adam Milliron.*

O'Halloran's Blarney Buster, created by Lenny O'Halloran of T.G.I.F. in Monroeville in March 1983. *Photo by Adam Milliron.*

The Rudy Judy, which was a popular drink at the Electric Banana. It was created by Judy Zarra, who co-owned the club. *Photo by Adam Milliron.*

Faust's Pact, from Fred Sarkis, was one of the more important drinks developed in the past decade in Pittsburgh's cocktail scene. *Photo by Adam Milliron.*

The Grass Skirt Goddess, from Greta Harmon. *Photo by Adam Milliron.*

Death's Comeback, from Spencer
Warren. *Photo by Adam Milliron.*

The Bladerunner, from Fred Sarkis. *Photo
by Adam Milliron.*

Post-Coital Embrace, from Carrie Clayton.
Photo by Adam Milliron.

Lagoonagroni, created by Sean Enright.
Photo by Adam Milliron.

Caramelized Onion & Gorgonzola Croquette with Mustard Cream Sauce, created by Monique Ruvolo. *Photo by Adam Milliron.*

Two women contemplate whether they should take a shot from the hip at Tequila Willies in 2001. *Photo by John Heller; copyright © Pittsburgh Post-Gazette, 2016, all rights reserved. Reprinted with permission.*

Dressed in leather, chains and spikes, Mark Dobosh, of Clairton, referred to himself as a mutt to the *Post-Gazette* and said he often haunts East Carson Street, where he found acceptance and attention. *Photo by Steve Mellon; copyright* © Pittsburgh Post-Gazette, *2016, all rights reserved. Reprinted with permission.*

A group of young women enjoy the nightlife at the popular Station Square club Rock Jungle when it was open. *Photo by John Heller; copyright* © Pittsburgh Post-Gazette, *2016, all rights reserved. Reprinted with permission.*

Tender Bar + Kitchen in Lawrenceville is emblematic of the transformation the once dilapidated neighborhood has undergone in the past two decades. *Photo by Bill Wade; copyright ©* Pittsburgh Post-Gazette, *2016, all rights reserved. Reprinted with permission.*

Butcher & the Rye in downtown Pittsburgh features one cocktail that costs more than $500. *Photo courtesy of the Rick DeShantz Restaurant Group.*

The Lava Lounge, the cocktail bar that started the recent renaissance, closed its doors in 2016. *Photo by Matt Freed; copyright ©* Pittsburgh Post-Gazette, *2016, all rights reserved. Reprinted with permission.*

A Metropol employee dances above the crowd on a Friday night at the club during the early 2000s. *Photo by Annie O'Neill; copyright* © Pittsburgh Post-Gazette, *2016, all rights reserved. Reprinted with permission.*

Joe Grushecky and the Houserockers perform at an Oakland club in the 1970s. *Photo courtesy of Joe Grushecky.*

From left to right, row one: Erika Joyner, Maggie Meskey and Jessica Keyser; *row two*: Sarah Williams, Nicole Battle and Kiersten Schilinski; *row three*: Heather Perkins, RaeLynn Harshman, Summer Voelker and Melissa Schafer; *row four*: April Diehl and Allie Contreras. *Photo by Julia Rendleman and Rebecca Droke; copyright* © Pittsburgh Post-Gazette, *2016, all rights reserved. Reprinted with permission.*

A line outside one of Tom and Maggie Jayson's discotheques in the 1970s. *Photo courtesy of Maggie Jayson.*

Some of the staff at one of the Jayson's clubs during the disco era. *Photo courtesy of Maggie Jayson.*

The view of Heaven, a nightclub in Pittsburgh, from a deejay's perspective in the 1980s. *Photo courtesy of Maggie Jayson.*

The floor of one of Tom and Maggie Jayson's nightclubs during their dominance in the 1970s and 1980s. *Photo courtesy of Maggie Jayson.*

Left: The Stanley Cup makes a stop at the Saloon in Mount Lebanon. Players had their own private pool room at the bar in the early 1990s. *Photo courtesy Jim Sheppard.*

Below: Shadyside attracted huge crowds during big events. When the Pirates won the World Series in 1971, many gathered on Walnut Street to celebrate. *Photo courtesy of Paul Corbett.*

on to Eleven Contemporary Kitchen, where he and other bartenders began experimenting with classics.

Rob Hirst was another bartender making waves. Hirst had stints at Mad Mex and Kaya before he moved to Soba, where he worked from 1996 to 1998. He reopened it in 2002. Hirst told *Pop City*, a weekly e-magazine in Pittsburgh, that he began to see a changing dining and drinking climate during the 1990s. In 1995, it was the waning days of the 1970s cocktails like Long Island iced teas, bay breezes and cosmopolitans.

Hirst has always had an educational approach to his bartending. Hirst wants to educate drinkers about different spirits, cocktails and the history. He has noticed how much the bartending mentality toward learning has changed.

"The throwback to the old craft, within the last 10 years, has come a long way," Hirst said in an interview with *Pop City*. "Within the last three years, it has blown up. You have to have educated bartenders who want to learn."

There was a rising contender to the South Side that would challenge its claim to being the most bohemian and hipster friendly neighborhood. Lawrenceville would undergo a dramatic transformation in the early part of the twenty-first century in Pittsburgh.

Part of that was due to the craft beer craze taking root toward the end of the 1990s. Despite the presence of local breweries, beer drinkers in Pittsburgh were largely shut out from most of the microbrews across the country.

Mad Mex, which was located in Oakland, opened in 1993. It offered only microbrews and Mexican brews. It had the beer trucked in from Allentown, which was three hundred miles away, according to a *Post-Gazette* article. It would set the trend toward craft beer drinking in the city, which would coincide with the craft cocktail revolution.

Bars began having more taps. Brewpubs sprang up around the city, and demand for creative takes on beer was just as high as the push for cleverly crafted cocktails. A keystone bar arose in Lawrenceville that led to the renaissance. It was the Church Brew Works, started by Sean Casey, a University of Colorado graduate who traveled the world as part of his work with his father's company.

Casey drank craft beers while in Colorado. He also had a number of beers and food while traveling throughout the world. Casey wanted to combine those experiences in his own business, so he opened Church Brew Works in 1996. He and some other investors bought the St. John the Baptist Church in Lawrenceville, which provided a uniquely religious beer-drinking experience. It had a European feel to it.

They were attracted to the church because it had easy parking and the neighborhood was affordable. They branded themselves with the Lawrenceville neighborhood by putting it under their banner and advertising it in promotional campaigns. Casey said there was a synergy between the two.

"We were very much an anchor restaurant, and we're in a very big building," Casey said over the phone. "So people became aware of the neighborhood and us. Even employees working in our place wanted to live here."

The neighborhood followed the same path the South Side did.

"As the neighborhood got better, more places popped up. But there are only a couple of places that have been open in Lawrenceville for twenty years," Casey said. "We've definitely helped identify the community and helped make ourselves a part of it."

Church Brew Works wasn't the only or even the first brewpub in the city. Penn Brewery, owned by Tom Pastorius, opened on the North Side in the 1980s. Three Rivers Brewing Company and Foundry Ale Works opened shortly after Church Brew.

The downtown area, particularly the cultural district, was revitalized in the twenty-first century largely because many upscale places set up shop there. Robin Fernandez opened the Bossa Nova in that neighborhood in 2001. It was a popular destination for influential people in the downtown industries.

"I built the Bossa Nova to have more of a lounge scene," Fernandez said. "There was a whole thing about being cool and having a bite to eat without having a meal. It became a meeting place. We designed it for the corporate scene. It was successful because of the corporate events. There were a lot of big-time movers and shakers."

Other bars would soon open downtown, including Seviche, which offered Latin food and cocktails. Most of the posh bars in Pittsburgh are located downtown as of 2015.

The cocktail revolution would take its biggest step when Fred Sarkis arrived. Sarkis, a drifter who picked up tricks of the bartending trade during his travels, came to Pittsburgh and revolutionized the way cocktails were made here. Sarkis was born in the Midwest, but he moved with his parents to a Canadian farm where he spent his childhood. When he turned sixteen, Sarkis moved to Toronto, where he got a job at a café. The restaurant eventually started to serve liquor, and that's when Sarkis got his start in bartending.

After Toronto, Sarkis moved to New York City, where he barbacked. Then he moved to Chicago in 2000. The cities influenced his interests. Since he worked daytime shifts, he spent the nights reading cocktail literature. After the bar he was working at in Chicago closed, he weighed his options. He was either going to move to Shanghai or to Pittsburgh to help Dok Harris run for mayor. He didn't get money for his campaign work, so he got a job at a little bar called Embury, which was owned by noted local bartender Spencer Warren. It was located in the Firehouse Lounge, also owned by Warren.

The Firehouse Lounge opened in 2004. Four years later, Embury was added to the first floor. The club had a speakeasy type of feel. There was no running water behind the bar, so the bartenders had to fill buckets of water to wash glassware. They served one wine by the glass. There was no beer or vodka offered at the Embury bar. But they had a list of ten featured house cocktails and a back catalogue of over one hundred classic cocktails.

Warren, of Mount Lebanon, graduated from the Kiski School in 1999. Then he went to Vanderbilt before transferring to Bucknell. His first foray in cocktails happened while tending bar at the fraternity functions that he organized while being its social chairman.

Warren and Sarkis met in Florida in 2009 and struck up a friendship. When Sarkis told him about his decision to go to Pittsburgh, Warren decided to offer him a job.

At his clubs, Warren decided to introduce fresh ingredients and fresh syrups. He had traveled to Milk and Honey in New York City, where he was impressed with the beverages he had with his girlfriend and friend. Warren gave Sarkis free rein over the menu.

"We brought him in, and he made some changes," Warren said. "We didn't carry vodka. He came in and tweaked it so that he came in with a new cocktail menu. I gave him carte blanche. It was just he and I. We were open the days he wanted to work."

Sarkis introduced fresh juices to cocktails. It was something he had done with his bartending when he discovered he preferred margaritas made with fresh ingredients rather than mixes. Sarkis also started a pre-Prohibition cocktail program. They didn't stock cranberry juice, vodka or Apple Pucker.

"What I thought would work was a corrective diet," Sarkis said. "The Firehouse had 27 flavors of vodka. So I tried to create something that was different in Pittsburgh so people could see the difference. It was so people would come in and try something different."

Sarkis attracted attention from the *Post-Gazette*. Cocktail critic Bill Toland heaped praise on Embury as one of the city's best, and few, handcrafted cocktail joints.

"Pittsburgh doesn't have a cocktail culture the way New Orleans, New York or Chicago does," Toland said. "There are lots of reasons for that: Pittsburgh has a reputation as a shot-and-beer town; Pennsylvania is a 'control state,' which makes it more difficult to get creative with your bar stock."

Toland speculated how the cocktail culture would evolve. "But all food-and-drink trends have a starting point," he said. "Think of the wine and Scotch lists that didn't exist 20 years ago at Pittsburgh restaurants; think of the popularity of craft beers."

Sarkis said that people change their habits once they see a better way of doing things. "Once you show people you could do something a little better, and there's no argument that fresh juice is better, from there, everything else happens," he said. "People start to go to places like that."

Egg whites became popular in Pittsburgh because of Sarkis and Warren. Part of that was because of Casey Hampton, nose tackle for the Steelers. Hampton walked into the bar one day and was looking for Warren. He asked for his favorite beer, which Sarkis didn't know. Sarkis had been washing glasses and was cleaning the fridge. He had his eggs out.

"He stopped me and said, 'Hey, what you got there? Can you make me a protein martini?' And he laughed at me, and I was about to put them away," Sarkis said over the phone. "But he said, 'No, make me a protein martini.' So I made him a Pisco sour. And he crushed it in almost his first sip. And his buddy wanted one, too. That became their thing. They would come in and ask for a drink with an egg. It became a thing."

Wine selections offered by restaurants diminished as cocktails became popular. In a 2011 article, *Post-Gazette* food critic China Millman said that people speculated as to why.

"High-end cocktails aren't exactly a bargain, but unlike wine, the labor of making the drink is typically visible and tangible to the drinker," Millman wrote. "Today's trendy cocktails typically include several liquors, as well as house-made mixers, infusions and garnishes. They're pretty and distinctive, not just another glass of red or white wine poured from a bottle."

The praise Sarkis received from the press attracted Enright's attention. Enright sent one of his protégés, Maggie Meskey, to see what Sarkis was doing.

Soon thereafter, Embury became the place for bartenders to go to. Embury fundamentally changed a culture that had struggled to develop the techniques needed to match up against New Orleans, New York City and Chicago.

"They were trying," Sarkis said. "But they didn't have any direction. It's one thing to see something and read about it. And it's another thing to experience it."

Summer Voelker, another rising bartender, came in as well and quickly made a name for herself, both in Pittsburgh and nationally when she was elected to participate in New Orleans Tales of the Cocktail as an apprentice.

Voelker, Meskey and other young bartenders would ask questions while visiting Embury. They would sit at the bar and listen to Sarkis explain how bartending should be done.

"If anyone tries something, I would give them the secret," Sarkis said. "Because it's all about changing the drinking culture. The more people taste fresh drinks, and practice proper techniques, the more people expect it. Being transparent makes people innovate."

Embury began to make a name nationally and attracted prominent bartenders to do guest shifts. Warren, Sarkis and Enright were proven names in bartending by that time. But Meskey, over the course of a half-decade, would become as equally well known. Meskey was from Lancaster County, in the heart of Amish country. In her time in the city, she has been praised for her larger-than-life persona. Her skill behind the bar would match her charisma.

Voelker and Meskey created a seasonally changing list of just six or seven cocktails that sold for ten dollars each. China Millman, the *Post-Gazette*'s food critic, said they were well-balanced and food-friendly drinks. The drinks included a sake cocktail, sprinkled with crushed pink peppercorns. Their creations went over well.

"Pittsburgh not only has an amazing new restaurant but also a new cocktail bar," Millman wrote in her review. "The whole program is impressive, but looking around the dining room one night, I wasn't a bit surprised that everyone seemed to be holding a cocktail glass."

Erika Joyner worked there as well. Jeremy Bustamante started there in October 2011. Bustamante began as a server and then worked his way up the ladder when Voelker left for a job at Harvard & Highland.

Bustamante said he thought the Salt of the Earth bar program was special because of its ambition and originality. It stood apart from other bars.

"It was basically Embury and Salt," Bustamante said over the phone. "A group of ladies led a charge. It's not surprising that it took a female perspective as an art form and as a craft. Women drove some of the earlier bartending culture. And that's started anew."

Meskey and Voelker brought attention to female bartenders. The *Post-Gazette* did a photo spread and article on female barkeeps in Pittsburgh reminiscent of the type Vogue gives its supermodels. In the photo, the bartenders—Erika Joyner, Sarah Williams, Meskey, April Diehl, Heather

Perkins, RaeLynn Harshman, Allie Conteras, Nicole Battle, Kiersten Schilinski, Jessica Keyser, Voelker and Melissa Schafer—represented the voice of the new Pittsburgh cocktail renaissance.

Voelker displayed deep passion for her craft, discussing the importance of craft research and honing the trade. While sexism was a serious topic of discussion in the article, Meskey gave the last word on the subject. "Our industry has an enormously supportive community here in Pittsburgh," she told the *Post-Gazette*. "I've also seen the same thing from my friends in the industry in bigger cities. We all know that we can grow and better ourselves and our careers by learning from our peers, our mentors and our role models."

Meskey also would become the first president of the Pittsburgh chapter of the United States Bartender's Guild. She, Voelker, Warren and Enright were the founding officers of the charter. The USBG chapter came about while Warren was visiting Tales of the Cocktail, a bartending educational fair held in New Orleans annually. He met the national head of the USBG, and they discussed the possibility of forming a chapter in Pittsburgh.

The USBG first set up in Philadelphia and included the city of Pittsburgh in it, making it Pennsylvania's USBG chapter. Warren and his crew weren't satisfied with that. So they pushed for a chapter in the western part of the state. They had to recruit a certain number of people to get the charter. They decided to do it through holding Punch socials at Embury.

"We needed at least 20 to 25 people. So we put out laptops and we said you got a free shot of Chartreuse," Warren said. "We drank a lot of Chartreuse. We had the largest signup in a day. So they gave us a temporary chapter. We got it because people paid $100 to drink Chartreuse all day. We were trying to get people to sign up."

The USBG provides opportunities to its members to travel across the country so they could keep up on the latest trends. Some, including Spencer Warren and Meskey, would earn high praise for the cocktails they introduced at events like Tales of the Cocktail. Pittsburgh bartenders impressed at such events.

"I think the USBG has definitely given people a lot more opportunities," Warren said. "People can learn a lot more about products. A lot more people will come in to do things. I used to have to fight to get reps and ambassadors in Pittsburgh. Now they want to come. They want to talk."

In the last few years, a number of critically acclaimed restaurants opened that were cocktail centric. Among them was Tender Bar + Kitchen, located in Lawrenceville. Owner Jeff Catalina recruited some of Pittsburgh's most

Stevie P, real name Stephen Pacacha, takes an innovative approach to pouring shots. Some bartenders in Pittsburgh are known for their flair. *Promotional photo courtesy Stephen Pacacha.*

respected bartenders to work there, according to the *Post-Gazette*: rum and Tiki-cocktail expert Craig Mrusek, cocktail educator Marie Perriello, Nathan Lutchansky, Sara Clarke, Sean Rosenkrans and Fred Arnold. The eclectic mix of talents made for a laboratory environment. All the bartenders had equal say in the shape the cocktail menu would take.

"All of our styles are different," Perriello told the *Post-Gazette*. "That's another thing we're doing that no one else has done in Pittsburgh."

Butcher & the Rye, in downtown Pittsburgh, has made the biggest waves nationally for its bar program. A staff led by Mike Mills, and later Spencer Warren, showcased how to make specialty whiskey–based cocktails. Butcher has an Old-Fashioned that costs upward of $500. One man in the city comes in frequently to order it.

In 2015, the people who operated Butcher opened täkō next door, which took the same approach to tequila that its predecessor took to whiskey. Meskey, who had been an original bartender at Butcher, was placed in charge of täkō's immense tequila program.

The bartenders are beginning to earn professional notoriety nationally. "We come up short at the James Beard awards," Sean Enright said. "But people always come away impressed when they see Pittsburgh bartenders at events such as Tales of the Cocktail or Portland Cocktail Week. I liken our cocktail scene to our music scene. We're insulated from the rest of the world, so we've developed our own unique style."

The ones who rise to the top are the bartenders who understand people. They are friends to the drinkers. "Only 10 percent can be great," Jimmy King said. "That's because of the personality. Bartenders with a good personality can get a job. Anyone can make 1,000 drinks. Respecting people is how you keep jobs."

Though personality remains the most important thing, the standard that bartenders are judged by has risen in the past twenty years largely because of their mastery of cocktails. "There's a different level of bartenders now," Warren said while sitting at the Beehive Coffeehouse on the South Side. "I go to a lot of places based on having a great cocktail. I want my bartenders to have a personality, but they have to make a good cocktail. I think the standard of what we eat and drink has risen. I think more so than anything, the standard has gone up in the past twenty years."

Faust Pact

Fred Sarkis, Embury, Pittsburgh

Fred Sarkis introduced Pittsburgh bartenders to the importance of measurement precision when he held court at Embury. This is arguably the cocktail that inspired Pittsburgh's current selection of craft bartenders to experiment with advancing techniques and trends.

1 slice jalapeño
3 dashes angostura bitters
2 ounces Bluecoat Gin
¾ ounce lemon juice
½ ounce basil syrup (recipe follows)
¼ ounce ginger syrup (recipe follows)

In a separate pint glass muddle jalapeño slice and angostura bitters. Strain juice into metal mixing tin but ensure the pepper does not get into tin by barring it with the end of the muddler. Add remaining ingredients and ice. Shake and double strain into chilled coupe glass. Serve up with pinch of cayenne on top.

Basil Syrup
6 ounces simple syrup
8 large basil leaves

Boil. Cool and refrigerate overnight. Strain.

Ginger Syrup
Peel fresh ginger with a spoon. Juice peeled ginger with a juicer machine and pour through a tea strainer into a measuring cup. Let ginger juice stand for 15 minutes or more. Using tea strainer again, mix equal parts ginger juice with equal parts sugar. Shake until sugar has dissolved.

PART II

WHO WE ARE AND THE DRINKS WE MAKE

8

THE STATESMAN

Photo by Adam Milliron.

Spencer Warren is still the guy younger generations of barkeeps go to when they want to learn the art of the craft cocktail. He's surrounded by bartenders from across the city during his Pop-Up Embury nights at Round Corner Cantina. Warren, in his late thirties, wants to preserve a tradition he helped establish in the past decade.

"It's nice that they come to me for advice," Warren said while making a drink at the bar. "I know how old I am. It's three generations asking about drinks now. A few people are intimidated because I'm a drink snob. I call a spade a spade."

Warren is still pushing the boundaries as a drink maker. But the recipes he developed early on still are as splashy as they were when he first created them. One of those from his early days is the Death's Comeback.

"It's the first real cocktail I made," Warren said. "Aside from martinis and the like. I was reading a bunch of cocktail books at the time. Maybe about twenty of them. You can come up with twenty drinks if you vary just one ingredient on a cocktail."

Death's Comeback
Spencer Warren, Embury

¾ ounce Bluecoat Gin
¾ ounce St. Germain Elderflower Liqueur
¾ ounce Aperol
½ ounce lime juice
¼ ounce simple syrup
3 drops absinthe

Combine ingredients in mixing tin with ice. Shake and double strain into a chilled coupe glass. Garnish with three drops of absinthe evenly spaced around the glass.

. . . .

Lagoonagroni
Sean D. Enright, Tiki Lounge

This cocktail is featured on the cover of this book.

1 ½ ounces Smith + Cross Rum
½ ounce banana-infused Wray + Nephew Overproof Rum (recipe follows)
¾ ounce pineapple and vanilla bean–infused Campari (recipe follows)
¾ ounce Antica Carpano Falernum (recipe follows)

Combine all ingredients in a shaker tin with ice. Shake and double strain into a coup glass. Garnish with orange peel.

Banana-Infused Wray + Nephew Overproof Rum
3 bananas, peeled and sliced
750-milliliter bottle Wray + Nephew Overproof Rum

Infuse for 3 days in a separate nonreactive container. Strain through cheesecloth.

Pineapple and Vanilla Bean–Infused Campari
3 vanilla beans, scored
1 pineapple, peeled and cut
750-milliliter bottle Campari

Infuse for 1 day in a separate nonreactive container. Remove the vanilla bean. Infuse for an additional 2 days. Strain through cheesecloth.

Antica Carpano Falernum
6 ounces absinthe
zest from 9 medium-sized limes
40 whole cloves
1½ ounces fresh ginger, peeled and julienned
¼ teaspoon almond extract
14 ounces Antica Carpano Formula Vermouth
4½ ounces fresh, strained lime juice

Combine first four ingredients in a jar and seal. Let soak for 24 hours. Strain through moistened cheesecloth, squeezing the solids to extract the last, flavorful bits of liquid. Add almond extract, Antica Carpano Formula vermouth and lime juice. Shake it all together and serve.

. . . .

The Apple Cort
Cortney Buchanan, Butcher and the Rye

1½ ounces Dalmore Small Batch Whisky
1 ounce Laird's Bonded Apple Brandy
½ ounce Nonino Amaro
¼ ounce demerara syrup
2 dashes Wigle Mole Bitters
1 dash angostura orange bitters

Combine ingredients in a mixing glass with ice and stir until well chilled and properly diluted. Strain over a large ice cube in a rocks glass. Garnish with an orange peel twist.

. . . .

The Atwood
Amanda Carto, Butterjoint

"A featured drink on Legume Bistro & Butterjoint's 2014 winter menu," says Carto.

¾ ounce Rittenhouse 100 Proof Bottled-In-Bond Straight Rye Whiskey
¾ ounce Calvados
¾ ounce yellow Chartreuse
1 spoon rich demerara syrup (2:1)
2 dashes orange bitters

Stir, strain into a chilled Nick & Nora glass. Express orange twist and discard.

. . . .

Bay of Biscay
John Pyles, Tender Bar & Kitchen

2 ounces cognac
½ ounce Cocchi Torino Vermouth
½ ounce Isastegi Cider syrup (recipe follows)
1 dash Bittermens Burlesque Bitters
1 spoon Lactart

Stir and strain into a chilled coupe. Garnish with a lemon twist.

Isastegi Cider Syrup
1 cup Isastegi Cider
1 cup demerara sugar
1 cup white sugar

Heat cider, demerara sugar and white sugar. Stir until combined. Never boil.

. . . .

Bebe's Sangria On Demand
Bethany Tryc, Tiki Lounge

2 ounces full-bodied red wine
1 ounce Maggie's Farm Spiced Rum
½ ounce triple sec
1½ ounces orange juice

Shake and roll into a hurricane glass. Top with Sprite. Garnish with chunks of orange and apple stirred into glass.

. . . .

Beet Around the Bush
RaeLynn Harshman, Dish Osteria

1½ ounces Boyd & Blair Vodka
½ ounce St. Germain Elderflower Liqueur
¾ ounce rosemary-lemon-beet shrub (recipe follows)
1 dash angostura bitters

Shake, double strain into a martini glass and garnish with rosemary sprig.

Rosemary-Lemon-Beet Shrub
5 red beets, peeled
1 cup apple cider vinegar
1 cup sugar
4 sprigs rosemary
1 teaspoon kosher salt
lemon juice equaling amount of beet juice extracted (about 2 cups)

Purée beets and vinegar. Strain. Should get about 2 cups. Combine the rest of the ingredients in a nonreactive bowl and let it steep for a day. Strain to discard any solids left in mixture.

. . . .

Beetlejuice
Andrea Davis, Spoon

2 ounces Tanqueray Gin
¼ ounce Campari
1 ounce beet simple syrup
½ ounce orange-clove water
¼ ounce lime juice

Combine all ingredients in a shaker tin with ice. Shake and double strain into a cocktail glass. Garnish with orange peel.

. . . .

Bixiou (Bitter Maiden)
Geoffrey Wilson, Embury

1 ½ ounces green Chartreuse
½ ounce Campari
½ ounce lime juice
½ ounce raspberry syrup
7 dashes Peychaud's Bitters

Shake and double strain over ice in a rocks glass.

. . . .

Black Tree
Craig Mrusek

1 ½ ounces El Dorado 12-Year Rum
¾ ounce Zirbenz Stone Pine Liqueur
¾ ounce Nux Alpina Walnut Liqueur
¼ ounce demerara syrup
6 drops Vieux Carré Absinthe

Stir everything with ice and strain into coupe. Garnish with small pinch of ground cloves on surface of drink.

Blood Orange Sour
Erika Clark, täkō

*1 ounce Ilegal Jóven Mezcal
1 ounce blood orange juice
½ ounce Solerno Blood Orange Liqueur
¼ ounce Campari
¾ ounce lemon juice
¾ ounce simple syrup
1 egg white*

Combine ingredients in a mixing tin without ice and dry shake vigorously. Add ice and shake a second time. Double strain into a chilled coupe glass. Garnish with 5 dashes Amargo Peruvian bitters.

. . . .

Brooklyn Bridge
Christopher Kuhn, Bar Marco

*1 ½ ounces Bulleit Rye
¾ ounce sweet vermouth
¼ ounce Maraschino Liqueur
¼ ounce Ramazotti Amaro
4 dashes chocolate bitters*

Build in a mixing glass. Fill with bar ice. Stir and strain into a coupe glass. Garnish with a maraschino cherry

. . . .

Casa Verde Margarita
Nathan Lutchansky, Verde Mexican Kitchen & Cantina

*2 ounces Pueblo Viejo Blanco Tequila
1 ounce Hiram Walker Orange Curaçao
¾ ounce lime juice*

Shake and strain into a rocks glass over ice. Salt rim, garnish with lime wedge.

PITTSBURGH DRINKS

· · · · · · · · · · · · · · · · · ·

The Cleanse
Salena Alexis Rebert Yetsko

1½ ounces Heaven Hill Bourbon
½ ounce Sortilege Maple Liqueur
¾ ounce lemon juice
1 spoon apple juice
2 dashes cayenne pepper

Combine ingredients in a mixing tin. Add ice and shake vigorously. Strain over ice in a pint glass. Top with water.

· · · · · · · · · · · · · · · · · ·

The Cocker Spaniel
Evan Swanson, Fire Side Public House

12 fresh mint leaves
2½ ounces Jameson Irish Whiskey
¼ ounce St. Germain Elderflower Liqueur
2 ounces cranberry juice
¾ ounce lime juice
¼ ounce simple syrup

Tear mint leaves and add to mixing tin with other ingredients. Shake and double strain into rocks glass. Garnish with lime wheel.

· · · · · · · · · · · · · · · · · ·

Copa De Fuego
Allieson Contreras

1 slice fresh jalapeño.
3 dashes angostura bitters
2 ounces Espolón Reposado Tequila
½ ounce Solerno Blood Orange Liquor
¾ ounce cardamom syrup
½ ounce lime juice

116

In a separate pint glass, muddle jalapeño slice and angostura bitters. Strain juice into metal mixing tin. Add remaining ingredients and ice. Shake and double strain into a coupe glass. Use a pinch of cayenne pepper on top to garnish.

9

THE REVOLUTIONARY

Photo by Pam Panchak; copyright © Pittsburgh Post-Gazette, 2016, all rights reserved. Reprinted with permission.

Fred Sarkis has a place among the greatest barkeeps in Pittsburgh's history. Like Joe Sala, Eddie Thomas or the beatnik bartenders of 1950s, he encapsulated his era of mixology. Without him, the craft cocktail renaissance of the past six years would never have happened. Sarkis's place reflected the importance of his profession throughout the city's history.

"Pittsburgh has always been a blue-collar town being built on the steel industry," Sarkis said over the phone. "It makes sense that bartenders are central to the lifestyles there. That's where a lot of those meetings happened—at a bar. And that can't happen without the bartender."

One of Sarkis's cocktails is the Bladerunner. Sarkis was trying to pair some unusual flavors with a different spirit. It's both familiar and unusual at the same time, he said. The name of the cocktail goes back to his obsession with detective noir films, including the Ridley Scott classic.

"I had this running joke of naming cocktails after fictional detectives," Sarkis said. "I would think of what they would drink. It was more of a discussion of whether he was a detective instead of a bounty hunter. In the movie, Harrison Ford plays a bladerunner. It plays out like a noir movie, but he's not really a detective."

The Bladerunner
Fred Sarkis

1 ½ ounces bourbon
¾ ounce Luxardo Amaro
½ ounce Hamilton Jamaican Rum
½ ounce Carpano Bianco Vermouth
2 dashes Bitter Cube Cherry Bark Vanilla Bitters
apple-infused olive oil

Combine the first five ingredients in a mixing glass with ice and stir until well chilled and properly diluted. Strain into a chilled coupe glass and garnish with several drops of apple-infused olive oil.

. . . .

The Crossing
Stephen "Stevie P." Pacacha

1 ½ ounces Mount Gay Aged Rum
¾ ounce Aztec Fire Chocolate Syrup (recipe follows)
1 ounce San Pellegrino Aranciata
2 dashes Fee Brothers Aztec Chocolate Bitters
1 dash orange bitters
Fill: 3 ounces Samuel Smith's Chocolate Stout

Combine ingredients in a cocktail tin with ice. Shake vigorously and double strain into a martini glass. Top with Samuel Smith's Chocolate Stout. Stir into cocktail. Garnish with orange zest.

Aztec Fire Chocolate Syrup
Aztec Fire Tea Blend from Teavana
sugar

Steep 5 to 6 mins. Add to sugar in a 1:1 ratio.

. . . .

The DFS No. 2
Giuseppe Capolupo, Bar Marco

2 ounces Amrut Old Port Deluxe Rum
¾ ounce Antica Carpano Formula Vermouth
¼ ounce orgeat
1 dash Bitter Truth Spiced Chocolate Bitters

Stir in mixing glass. Strain into a chilled coupe glass. Garnish with a cherry.

. . . .

The Dutchess
Derek Whitten

1½ ounces Early Grey Tanqueray Gin (recipe follows)
¼ ounce Aperol
½ ounce strawberry-fennel shrub (recipe follows)
½ ounce lemon juice
¼ ounce agave
2 dashes Peychaud's Bitters

Combine ingredients in a mixing tin and add ice. Shake, double strain over large ice cube in a rocks glass. Express lemon oils over the glass and add peel to cocktail to garnish.

Early Grey Tanqueray Gin
3 tablespoons loose-leaf Early Grey oolong tea per every 12 ounces of gin

Stir vigorously for 3 minutes and then let sit for 5 minutes. Shake contents before straining and bottling.

Strawberry-Fennel Shrub
2 cartons of strawberries, halved
2 fennel bulbs
1 teaspoon fennel seed
1:1 sugar vinegar (balsamic)

Cook over medium heat for 20 minutes. Let sit overnight and then strain. Best served after 1½ months.

Falling for Dutch
Dutch DeVries, USBG Pittsburgh

1 ½ ounces Bols Barrel Aged Genever
1 ounce Rothman & Winters Apricot Liqueur
¾ ounce lemon juice
½ ounce fall spice rich syrup (recipe follows)
1 egg white

Add ingredients to a shaker tin and dry shake. Add ice and shake until chilled. Double strain into a chilled egg coupe glass. Garnish with a dust of ground cinnamon/nutmeg blend.

Fall Spice Rich Syrup
1 cup water
2 cups pure cane sugar
5 peppercorns
5 cardamom pods
4 cinnamon sticks, crushed
5 cloves
2 twists of orange peel
½ vanilla bean, sliced open (or ¼ teaspoons vanilla extract)

Simmer all ingredients in a pan for 30 minutes (don't boil); strain through a cheesecloth and let thoroughly cool before bottling.

. . . .

Fat Elvis
Monika McAndrew & Marty Schwab, Lava Lounge

1 ½ ounces vanilla vodka
1 ounce 99 Bananas
½ ounce Frangelico
½ ounce Reese's Pourable Peanut Butter
½ ounce cream

Combine ingredients in a mixing tin. Add ice and shake vigorously. Double strain into a martini glass rimmed with bacon bits dust.

. . . .

PITTSBURGH DRINKS

Frasier

Sarah Walsh, Caffè d'Amore Coffee Company

1 ½ ounces Boyd & Blair Vodka
1 ½ ounces almond milk
1 ½ ounces cold-brew coffee (recipe follows)
¾ ounce vanilla syrup

Combine ingredients in a mixing tin with ice and shake vigorously. Strain over fresh ice in a Collins glass.

Cold-Brew Coffee

⅓ cup medium-coarse ground coffee
1 ½ cups cold water

Mix ingredients together in a jar. Cover and let rest at room temperature for 12 hours or overnight. Strain twice through a coffee filter, a fine-mesh sieve or a sieve lined with cheesecloth.

. . . .

Gastaldi Sunrise

Brian Gastaldi, Dish Osteria

"Makes it feel extra special done tableside," says Gastaldi.

1 ½ ounces José Cuervo Tradicional Silver
1 ½ ounces orange juice
½ ounce Dolin Rouge Vermouth
½ ounce Dolin Dry Vermouth

Quick shake the ingredients and strain over good ice in a rocks glass. Express a nice orange peel over top, present to your guest and drizzle ½ ounce Campari slowly on top.

Gimlet-Eyed Girl

Greta Harper

2 ounces 42 Below Vodka
¼ ounce Don Ciccio & Figli Fennel Liqueur
¾ ounce lemon juice
½ ounce simple syrup
4 basil leaves

Tear basil leaves and combine ingredients in a mixing tin with ice. Shake and strain into an ice-filled Collins glass. Garnish with basil leaf.

. . . .

Golden Years

Summer Voelker

1 ¼ ounces Wigle Ginever
¼ ounce Royal Combier
½ ounce Dolin Blanc
1 ¼ ounces pineapple juice
1 ounce cucumber juice

Combine ingredients in a mixing tin with ice. Shake and double strain into a chilled coupe glass.

. . . .

Guilty Rose

Fred Sarkis, Embury

½ ounce Campari
2 ounces Hendricks's Gin
½ ounce St. Germain Elderflower Liqueur
½ ounce lemon juice
½ ounce simple syrup

Prepare your serving wine glass by adding ice and Campari to the glass. Set aside. In a mixing tin, add remaining ingredients with ice. Shake vigorously. Dump the Campari-soaked ice from your wine glass. Double strain cocktail from the mixing tin into your Campari-rinsed glass. Add 3 drops of Peychaud's Bitters on top.

. . . .

Green

Jessicarobyn Keyser, Union Pig & Chicken

1½ ounces liquor of choice (optional)
4 ounces The Best Lemonade (recipe follows)
1 ounce Green Juice (recipe follows)

Shake and roll rocks into a Collins glass (or a jelly jar). Garnish with a sprig of cilantro.

The Best Lemonade

zest strips from 12 lemons and 2 grapefruits
1½ cups sugar
3 cups lemon juice
½ cup honey
3 quarts water

Toss zest and sugar together in a glass or metal container. Muddle gently until you see the oils begin to extract, and then allow to sit, stirring or agitating occasionally, for at least 6 hours and no more than 24. Add the citrus juice to the oleo saccharum and stir to ensure that all sugar is dissolved, if it wasn't already. Add the honey, and stir until fully incorporated. Add water, stir and strain to remove strips of zest. Should make about 1 gallon.

Green Juice

2 quarts water
1 standard bunch cilantro (usually about ¼ pound), washed very thoroughly, all browned leaves and thickest parts of the stems removed
4 green jalapeños, washed, stems and seeds removed

Cut all produce into 1-inch lengths and place all ingredients into a high-speed blender (you may need to do this in batches). Purée until totally liquefied and then strain through fine mesh. If not using immediately, add a few drops of spirulina, chlorophyll or algae extract (all are usually found in the nutritional supplements section of places like the Co-op and Whole Foods) to preserve and intensify the bright green color. Keyser says, "Alternatively, cheat and use green food dye, because that shit is just fine."

· · · · · · · · · · · · · · · · · ·

The Harrison
Phil Ward, The Rowdy Buck

1 ounce Rittenhouse Rye
1 ounce Laird's Straight Apple Brandy Bottled in Bond
¼ ounce Medley Number 3 (recipe follows)
1 dash angostura bitters

Stir in mixing glass with ice. Strain over large ice cube in an Old-Fashioned glass. Garnish with orange twist.

Medley Number 3
2 parts El Dorado 12-Year Rum
1 part ginger syrup
1 part cinnamon bark syrup

Mix all ingredients in a sealable jar.

· · · · · · · · · · · · · · · · · ·

Hattori Hanzo
Collin McNamee, Soba/Umi

1 ½ ounces Bluecoat Gin
¾ ounce Fino Sherry
1 ounce crabapple cider
½ ounce demerara syrup
½ ounce yuzu juice

Shake with ice and double strain into chilled coupe glass. Garnish with skewered halved crabapple.

· · · · · · · · · · · · · · · · · ·

Island Port
April Diehl, Embury

1 ½ ounces Sandeman Port
½ ounce Smith + Cross Jamaican Rum
¾ ounce cinnamon syrup
¾ ounce lemon juice
½ ounce ginger syrup

Shake, strain over ice. Top with soda water. Lemon peel garnish.

. . . .

Jameskiller
James Morrow, Tiki Lounge

¾ ounce Don Q Cristal Rum
¾ ounce Sailor Jerry Rum
¾ ounce Myers Rum
¾ ounce Kahlua
½ ounce Wray & Nephew Overproof Rum
1 ounce coconut cream
1 ounce pineapple juice

Combine all ingredients in a mixing tin. Shake well. Pour unstrained into pilsner glass filled with ice. Garnish with pineapple, cherry, lime wheel and other Tiki accoutrements.

. . . .

Juggling Coconuts
Mai Jeans, The Commoner

1 ½ ounces coconut-washed Espolón Blanco Tequila (recipe follows)
½ ounce Cointreau
½ ounce cucumber sherbet (recipe follows)
½ ounce lime juice

Combine ingredients in mixing tin. Add ice. Shake and strain over fresh ice into a rocks glass. Garnish with a cucumber slice.

Coconut-Washed Tequila
750 milliliters tequila
15 ounces organic, unrefined coconut oil

Pour the tequila into a 6-liter cambro, a large swing-top jar or any nonreactive container that can hold at least 4 liters. Melt the coconut oil and make sure it's is really hot. Pour coconut oil into tequila and cover. Shake vigorously. Shake twice for about 5 minutes no more than 3 minutes apart. Let the tequila sit at room temperature for 8 hours. Put into the freezer for 4 hours, until the coconut oil is solid and can be removed in one clean piece. Once the coconut oil has been removed let the tequila come to room temperature. Strain through a chamois and then through a chamois lined with a coffee filter.

Cucumber Sherbet
1 English cucumber about 10 inches long
1½ cups sugar
12 ounces cucumber juice

Thinly slice cucumber and combine with sugar in a large bowl. Lightly muddle, put into a plastic bag and vacuum seal it as if you were starting an oleo saccharum. In about 45 minutes, it will start to liquefy. Over medium heat in a medium saucepan, combine cucumber oleo and cucumber juice. Stir until any remaining sugar is dissolved and simmer for about 5 minutes. Strain through a chamois and let cool.

. . . .

Juicy Pepper
Olga Brindar, Club Café

1½ ounces Espolón Reposado Tequila
¾ ounce Midori
½ ounce lime juice
½ ounce hot pepper simple syrup (recipe follows)

Rim a chilled martini glass with cayenne pepper. Combine ingredients in a mixing tin. Add ice. Shake and double strain into glass. Serve. Burn your mouth off and love it. Keeps the demons away!

Hot Pepper Simple Syrup
Chop jalapeños and simmer over low flame with equal parts water and organic cane sugar for about ten minutes. Strain and let cool. Brindar recommends, "Use [hot pepper simple syrup] with wild abandon."

. . . .

The Katharine
Sarah Anne Clarke

2 ounces Elijah Craig 12-Year Bourbon
1 ounce Byrrh Grand Quinquina
½ ounce Super Punch Jannamico
2 dashes Bitterman's Burlesque Bitters
1 dash Bitterman's Tiki Bitters
1 dash coffee tincture (recipe follows)

Add ingredients to a mixing glass and add ice. Stir and strain into a chilled coupe glass. Garnish with a fancy cherry and an additional three drops of coffee tincture on surface of drink.

Coffee Tincture
Add 2 tablespoons lightly ground coffee beans to 4 ounces Rittenhouse 100-Proof Rye Whiskey in a mason jar. Cover and let sit 1 month, agitating often. "Headstrong and sophisticated," says Clarke.

. . . .

Kentuck Knob
Alyssa McGrath

1 ounce Lustau Solera Sherry
1 ounce Old Overholt Rye Whiskey

1 ounce Amaro Montenegro
¼ ounce simple syrup
¼ ounce lemon juice

Shake and double strain into a rocks glass over a big cube. Garnish with lemon twist.

. . . .

Kiss from a Rose
Ruth Ann Tatar

2 ounces Laird's Applejack
¼ ounce Ancho Reyes Ancho Chile Liqueur
¾ ounce lemon juice
½ ounce grenadine
½ ounce cinnamon syrup
2 dashes Wigle Mole Bitters

Combine ingredients in a shaker tin filled with ice and shake vigorously. Double strain into a chilled coupe glass. Express the oil from a lemon peel on top of the cocktail and perfume the glass. Wrap peel around apple slice and spear with pick for the garnish.

. . . .

Kumquat Caipirinha
Michel Mincin

½ ounce lime juice
4 kumquats, halved
3 tablespoons brown sugar
¼ teaspoon grated ginger
3 ounces cachaça

Muddle all ingredients in a mixing tin, except for cachaça. Add ice and cachaça, shake and roll entire cocktail into a rocks glass.

10

THE EVERYWHERE GIRL

Photo by Adam Milliron.

At Hidden Harbor, a tiki bar in Squirrel Hill, Greta Harmon makes tropical drinks while Caribbean music plays in the background. Harmon fits in here, as she fits in anywhere. She's worked in all kinds of bars throughout western Pennsylvania, including Meat & Potatoes in downtown Pittsburgh.

"I took the things I learned at one place and took it to another," Harmon said while making an island drink. "I tried to learn as much as I could from the people who I worked with in those bars."

Harmon moved to Pittsburgh when she started junior high school. She has worked at a college sports bar in Johnstown, Bar Louie in Station Square, Redbeard's and Mullen's on the North Shore.

Her Grass Skirt Goddess is a concoction that would do as well in Negril or Montego Bay as it does in Pittsburgh.

In a city with as much connection to the Caribbean as Pittsburgh—with the Cuban barkeeps who came in the 1930s and 1940s—Harmon has helped reestablish the tiki trend with her drink.

"It's a fun, groovy, strong drink," Harmon said. "Like most great drinks, it'll transport you from cold, rainy and dreary Pittsburgh to somewhere tropical."

Grass Skirt Goddess

Greta Harmon

1 ounce Cruzan Aged Light Rum
1 ounce Appleton Rum
½ ounce Lemon Hart 151 Demerara Rum
1 ounce passion fruit juice
1 ounce falernum
1 ounce grapefruit juice
2 ounces pineapple juice
1 ounce demerara syrup

Combine ingredients in a mixing tin. Add ice, shake and strain over ice into tiki mug.

. . . .

Lady in Red

Curtis Thornton, Grit & Grace

2 ounces Common Decency Gin
½ ounce Campari
1 ounce orgeat
½ ounce ginger beer
¼ ounce lemon juice
1 egg white

Combine ingredients in mixer tin and dry shake. Add ice and shake vigorously. Strain into an egg coupe. Using a mister, spray angostura bitters over a lit match over the top of the cocktail.

. . . .

La Muerta Gris

Lucky Munro

2 ounces Sangre de Vida Blanco Tequila
¾ ounce orgeat
½ ounce lemon juice

¼ ounce Art in the Age Sage Liqueur
¼ ounce Luxardo Maraschino
pinch salt
pinch activated charcoal

Combine ingredients in mixing tin. Add ice and shake vigorously. Double strain into chilled coupe glass.

. . . .

Long Thyme Coming
Cat Cannon, Wallace's TapRoom

"I love plays on words, and I love Bruce Springsteen. I brought these two passions together in the name of this cocktail. Thyme is one of the ingredients, and 'Long Time Coming' is a favorite Springsteen song of mine," says Cannon.

1 ounce cardamom-infused vodka (recipe follows)
1 ounce grapefruit-thyme oleo saccharum (recipe follows)
½ ounce Campari
Fill: champagne

Shake ingredients and double strain into champagne flute. Top with champagne and garnish with thyme sprig and grapefruit peel.

Cardamom-Infused Vodka
5 lightly crushed cardamom pods
1 bottle vodka

Combine ingredients. Let sit 2 to 3 days, depending on desired flavor profile. Strain out cardamom.

Grapefruit-Thyme Oleo Saccharum
peels of 3 grapefruits
5 thyme sprigs
1 cup sugar

When peeling the grapefruit, make sure not to include any white pith. Add peels and thyme sprigs to a large nonreactive bowl. Cover peels and thyme with sugar and let sit overnight. Oil from peels should express into sugar, creating a citrus oil. Gently muddle peels to release remaining oils. Let sit for one hour more. Strain off the sugar oil from the peels and thyme. Save peels for garnish.

. . . .

Lost to Adeline
Carrie Clayton, The Livermore

1 ¼ ounces Manzanilla Sherry
1 ¼ ounces Plymouth Gin
½ ounce thyme-infused Bauchant
1 dash grapefruit bitters

Stir and strain into a chilled coupe. Garnish with a grapefruit peel.

. . . .

Marceline
Dani Erdos-Kramer, Bar Marco

1 ½ ounces Hendricks Gin
½ ounce Campari
½ ounce Super Punch Jannamico
½ ounce Cointreau

Stir in mixing glass. Strain into a chilled coupe. Serve up with orange twist garnish.

. . . .

Marie An' Fernet
Marie Frances Perriello

1 pinch salt
2 lemon wedges

1 ½ ounces Carpano Antica Formula
½ ounce Fernet Branca
¼ ounce lemon juice

Muddle salt with lemon wedges. Add remaining ingredients and shake hard with ice. Strain over crushed ice in rocks glass. Garnish with a mint sprig.

. . . .

Moneda Del Muerto
J. "Skoob" Kull

1 ounce Vida Mezcal Jóven
¾ ounce Cointreau
½ ounce ginger syrup
¼ ounce lemon juice
4 dashes peach bitters

Combine ingredients in mixing tin. Add ice and shake vigorously. Double strain into a chilled coupe glass. Garnish with an orange peel.

. . . .

Nasty Nasherita
Byron Nash, Harris Grill

3 ounces Reposado Tequila
¾ ounce Cointreau
1 ounce Grand Marnier
1 ounce lime juice
½ ounce simple syrup

Shake vigorously and strain over fresh ice in a pint glass. Garnish with a lime wheel.

. . . .

No Expectations

Chelsea Colby, Il Tetto in Sienna Mercato

1 ounce Bluecoat Gin
½ ounce Trader Vic's Macadamia Liqueur
½ ounce Cocchi Barolo Chinato
½ ounce demerara syrup (1:1)
½ ounce lemon juice
¼ ounce fresh pineapple Juice
1 egg white
3 dashes Fee Brothers Cardamom Bitters

Add all ingredients to a shaker. Dry shake. Add ice and shake again. Double strain into a chilled coupe glass. Express a lemon peel over the drink and discard.

. . . .

Nori by Nature

Danielle Skapura, Acacia

1 ounce Dolin Veritable Genepy Des Alpes
½ ounce Bombay East Gin
¾ ounce Nori Tincture (recipe follows)
½ ounce lime juice
½ ounce ginger syrup

Combine ingredients in a shaker tin and shake vigorously. Double strain into a chilled coupe.

Nori Tincture

Infuse nori edible seaweed in a bottle of Stolichnaya 100-proof vodka. Let sit for 12 hours or overnight. Strain through cheesecloth and rebottle into a clean pour bottle.

. . . .

Novocaine

J. Endress

1 ½ ounces butter-infused Stonewall Rum (recipe follows)
½ ounce Ramazzotti Amaro
1 ½ ounces orange juice
½ ounce Coco Lopez Cream of Coconut
1 pinch kosher salt
1 dash Mozart Chocolate Bitters

Shake and strain into an empty double rocks glass. Heap with crushed ice. Shave chocolate over the top with a microplane.

Butter-Infused Stonewall Rum

2 750-milliliter bottles Stonewall Rum
¼ pound unsalted butter

Pour rum into a 4-quart cambro. Melt unsalted butter and pour it into the cambro with the rum. Mix thoroughly; then store in the freezer for 24 hours. Strain through a fine-mesh strainer and then through a coffee filter. Bottle for use. Recipe should make just under 1.5 liters

. . . .

The Old-Fashioned Bar Brawl

Jayelle Cumberledge, Tiki Lounge

1 orange half wheel
¼ ounce Campari
¼ ounce simple syrup
½ ounce Barrow's Intense Ginger Liqueur
2 ounces Jameson Irish Whiskey

Muddle orange with Campari, simple syrup and ginger liqueur. Add Jameson and shake with ice. Double strain into a chilled martini glass. Garnish with lime peel.

. . . .

Old Westsylvanian
Jill Steiner, Wigle Whiskey

"A smoky, smooth, Pennsylvania bourbon Old-Fashioned," says Steiner.

2 ounces Wigle Organic Yellow Corn Bourbon
½ ounce Russian Caravan simple syrup (recipe follows)
2 to 3 dashes Wigle Organic Pomander Orange Bitters

Build in a rocks glass over large ice cube. Stir for 30 seconds. Garnish with a wide orange peel after expressing oil over glass to release zest.

Russian Caravan Simple Syrup

Steep 2 tablespoons Russian Caravan tea into 1 cup heated simple syrup. Let steep for 5 minutes; then strain.

. . . .

Once Upon a Time in Shaolin
Will Groves, Smallman Galley

1 ¼ ounces Momokawa Organic Junmai Sake
¾ ounce Carpano Antica Formula
½ ounce Cynar
½ ounce Aperol

Build over large ice cube in an Old-Fashioned glass. Garnish with an entire orange peel, curled into a rose, on a bamboo cocktail pick.

. . . .

Philotes Cup
Sean D. Enright, Spoon

"Philotes is the Greek spirit of friendship, affection and sexual intercourse," says Enright.

1 ounce green Chartreuse
1 ounce Averna Amaro
1 ounce Skinos Mastiha
½ ounce simple syrup
½ ounce lemon juice
Fill: club soda

Add all the ingredients to a mixing tin with ice. Shake vigorously and strain over fresh ice in a tall Collins glass. Fill with soda. Garnish with spanked mint.

. . . .

The PiXburgh Kid
Timothy Garso, Smallman Galley

"This cocktail comes from the Smallman Galley Spring 2016 cocktail menu, which was all Pittsburgh Pirates themed/puns. It was inspired by two main things: my love of all things sherry and our recently departed homegrown kid, Neil Walker," says Garso.

1 ounce Lustau Pedro Ximenez Sherry
1 ounce Stonewall Rum
¾ ounce Atxa Vino Vermouth Bianco
½ ounce lemon juice
3 dashes angostura bitters

Combine ingredients in a mixing tin. Add ice, shake and double strain in a chilled coupe glass. Garnish with a lemon twist.

. . . .

Pizzelle Cocktail

Elliott Sussman, Tender Bar + Kitchen

1 ¼ ounces Dolin Dry Vermouth
1 ounce Feretti Biscotti Liqueur
⅔ ounce Efe Raki
2 dashes Regan's Orange Bitters

Stir, and strain into a rocks glass over a large ice cube. Garnish with an orange peel and star anise bulb.

. . . .

Prairie Fire

Shane Morrison, Prairie

1 rosemary sprig
¼ ounce green Chartreuse
1 ½ ounces Old Forester Signature Bourbon
½ ounce honey syrup
½ ounce Lillet Blanc
½ ounce lemon juice

Smack a 3-inch sprig of rosemary and drop in coupe glass. Pour green Chartreuse over sprig and set aside. In a mixing tin combine bourbon, honey syrup, Lillet and lemon juice. Add ice and shake vigorously. Light Chartreuse on fire in glass; then douse by double straining cocktail over the flame.

11

THE CHESS PLAYER

C arrie Clayton moves about the circular bar at Poros, an establishment in Market Square typical of the more upscale places downtown. She's characteristic of the city's barkeeps—smart, understated and personable. But she's contemplating her moves carefully.

"When I'm at a bar, I like the mental game of chess we play," Clayton said as she moved around the room. "It's shuffling around to keep the customers happy. My favorite guests are those that come in miserable. Making them happy is fulfilling."

Clayton has lived around the country, including stints in New York City, where she worked at a dive bar in Brooklyn. She left there because backroom cocaine deals were happening while she worked. She moved back to Pittsburgh in 2006 and worked at another dive bar in Natrona Heights. During that time, she amassed a library of cocktail books. And she visited Embury Lounge frequently. Clayton broke into the Pittsburgh market by landing a bartending job at Bar Marco before moving on to Sonoma Grille.

Photo by Adam Milliron.

One of her favorite drinks to make is the Post-Coital Embrace. The drink has an interesting backstory.

"At a restaurant I worked at, I had a conversation about appropriately named drinks," Clayton said. "But we started talking about drinks you wanted to have after sex. And the Post-Coital Embrace reflects that."

Post-Coital Embrace

Carrie Clayton, The Livermore

1 ounce Pedro Romero Fino Sherry
½ ounce Crème Yvette
½ ounce Barrow's Intense Ginger Liqueur
½ ounce Benedictine

Stir and strain into a sherry glass.

. . . .

Ramon's Gin Fizz

Maggie Meskey

¼ avocado sliced
¾ ounce lemon juice
¾ ounce lime juice
2 ounce Matcha Green Tea–Infused Tanqueray Gin (recipe follows)
1 ounce heavy whipping cream
¾ ounce rich demerara syrup (2:1)
3 drops rose water
3 ounces chilled Jarritos Mandarin soda

Combine the avocado and lemon and lime juices into a mixing tin and muddle. Add remaining ingredients to the tin with ice and shake vigorously. Pour the Jarritos Mandarin soda into a Collins glass. Using a both a Hawthorne and tea strainer, carefully double strain the contents of the shaker into the glass of soda, pouring the mixture directly down the center. Using a microplane, grate some orange zest over the top of the drink, add a straw and serve.

Matcha Green Tea–Infused Tanqueray Gin

Add matcha green tea to gin, agitate and strain after 24 hours.

. . . .

Red Pepper
Round Corner Cantina

1 tablespoon chopped red bell pepper
1 pinch black pepper
4 basil leaves
½ ounce lemon juice
1 ½ ounces Espolón Blanco Tequila
½ ounce St. Germain Elderflower Liqueur
½ ounce simple syrup
½ ounce green Chartreuse

Muddle red pepper, black pepper, basil and lemon juice in mixing tin. Add tequila, St. Germain and simple syrup to the tin with ice and shake. Drizzle green Chartreuse into shaker and double strain into coupe glass. Garnish with chile de árbol.

· · · · · · · · · · · · · · · · · · · ·

Red Velvet Swing
Don Bistarkey, Lava Lounge

"Commissioned by LUPEC [Ladies United for the Preservation of Endangered Cocktails] for their 2001 Honoree Evelyn Nesbit, a famous (infamous) chorus girl from the early twentieth century, whose sexual assault by an older New York socialite led to her jealous husband murdering him and a subsequent 'Trial of the Century' in 1906," says Bistarkey.

1 sugar cube
½ ounce pomegranate molasses
2 drops rose water
5 ounces chilled champagne, divided

In mixing glass combine sugar cube, pomegranate molasses and a few drops of water. Muddle. Add 1 ounce of champagne to mixing glass. Stir until sugar is dissolved. Add ice and stir until well chilled. Add remaining 4 ounces of champagne to chilled flute. Slowly strain contents of mixing glass into flute. Float 2 drops rose water atop cocktail. Garnish with cherry, edible flower and pomegranate seed.

· · · · · · · · · · · · · · · · · · · ·

Rhus Juice

Lynn Falk & Shane Morrison, Acacia

2 ounces Bluecoat Gin
1 ounce heavy cream
¾ ounce sumac syrup
¾ ounce lemon juice
2 spoon quince preserves
1 egg white
Fill: club soda

Dry shake. Add ice and shake. Strain into a Collins glass. Top with soda.

. . . .

Root Champarelle

Spencer Warren, Firehouse Lounge/Embury

¾ ounce Courvoisier Cognac
¾ ounce orange curaçao
¾ ounce yellow Chartreuse
½ ounce root liqueur
½ ounce lemon juice
½ ounce simple syrup
1 dash angostura bitters

Combine ingredients in a mixing tin. Add ice, shake and strain over fresh ice in a copper mug. Garnish with a mint sprig.

. . . .

Sailor's Warning

Greta Harmon, 2014 Pittsburgh Cocktail Week

"Winner 'Best Cocktail' 2014 Pittsburgh Cocktail Week," says Greta Harmon.

1 ½ ounces Del Maguey Vida Mezcal
½ ounce yellow Chartreuse
2 ounces orange juice
½ ounce lime juice

143

Combine ingredients in a mixing tin. Add ice, shake and double strain into cocktail glass. Pour ½ ounce crème de cassis into the side of the glass and allow to sink to bottom of cocktail. Garnish with orange peel.

. . . .

Scarlet Begonia
Rob McCaughey, Pittsburgh Cocktail Week

1 ½ ounces Hendrick's Gin
½ ounce Ferriera White Port
¼ ounce Maraschino Liqueur
¼ ounce Cointreau
1 dash orange bitters

Stir all ingredients in a mixing glass with ice and strain into a chilled coupe. Pour a ¼ ounce of sparkling shiraz into the center of the cocktail. Garnish with an edible flower.

12

THE ENTHUSIAST

Photo by Adam Milliron.

Rob Ricci has moved up in the local beverage industry in the past few years. Presently, he is the head distiller at Boyd & Blair. But he still bartends occasionally because it's in his blood. He's emblematic of how passionate barkeeps in the city are about running and improving the cocktail scene in Pittsburgh.

Ricci thinks understanding the city's heritage is vital to city's future nightlife. "Once you know that, then you can put your own spin on it," he said. "Looking back on our history is how this whole revolution got started."

Ricci, of Friendship, Pennsylvania, has bartended for thirteen years. He got into craft cocktails while at Spoon, which he began working at in 2011. He has developed a number of cocktails over the years, including the London Calling.

"It's refreshing," Ricci said. "It's light, but also complex. I made it a few years ago, and I think it holds up. It works well in the summer."

London Calling
Robert M. Ricci, Boyd & Blair Vodka Distillery, Glenshaw

¾ ounce Boyd & Blair Vodka
¾ ounce lavender-infused Boyd & Blair Vodka (recipe follows)
½ ounce Pimm's No. 1 Cup
½ ounce lemon juice
½ ounce simple syrup
Fill: Fuller's ESB

Shake all ingredients together, except beer. Strain over fresh ice. Top with beer to fill. Add garnish.

Lavender-Infused Vodka
750 milliliters Vodka
3 sprigs lavender

In a nonreactive vessel, mix vodka with lavender. Let sit for 7 days. Strain and serve.

. . . .

Senti Correcto
Rob Ricci, Senti Restaurant & Wine Bar

1 ounce Casa Motore Grappa
1 ounce American coffee
1 ounce chicory syrup (recipe follows)
1 ounce heavy cream

Shake all ingredients vigorously with ice. Strain into footed mug.

Chicory Syrup
1 cup hot water
1 cup sugar
2 tablespoons ground chicory

Mix hot water with sugar and ground chicory. Dissolve sugar in water; steep chicory for 15 minutes. Strain with fine mesh strainer and then a coffee filter.

. . . .

Sergeant Pepper's Old Fashioned
Mike Mills, Meat & Potatoes

"This cocktail, I believe, exposed more 'non-whiskey' drinkers to bourbon than any specific cocktail in Pittsburgh. It's been on the Meat & Potatoes cocktail menu for four years now and is considered a staple in the restaurant," says Mills.

2 ounces Bulleit Bourbon
½ ounce BPT (black pepper and thyme) syrup (recipe follows)
2 dashes Fee Bros. Whiskey Barrel Bitters

Combine all ingredients in a mixing glass. Add ice and stir until well chilled. Strain into a rocks glass over large ice cube. Garnish with lemon peel.

BPT Syrup
3 cups white sugar
3 cups water
6 tablespoons fresh-ground black pepper
10 to 12 large sprigs thyme

In a saucepan, combine white sugar and water. Stir and put on low heat until all sugar is dissolved. Add black pepper and thyme. Simmer for 10 to 15 minutes, until the thyme is fully infused. Next, take the syrup off heat and let cool for 30 to 45 minutes. Strain through cheesecloth until pepper debris is not visible.

. . . .

Smoking Jacket

Max Stein, Independent Brewing Company

1 ½ ounces Laird's Bonded Apple Brandy
¼ ounce Laphroaig 10 Year Scotch Whisky
¼ ounce rich toasted vanilla demerara syrup
4 to 5 dashes Bar Keep Apple Bitters

Build in rocks glass. Stir with large ice cube. Garnish with a piece of vanilla bean and flamed orange peel.

. . . .

Spring Roll

Nicole Battle

1 ¼ ounces Shochu
¼ ounce yellow Chartreuse
¾ ounce lemongrass syrup (recipe follows)
½ ounce yuzu

Combine all ingredients in a mixing tin. Add ice, shake vigorously and strain over fresh ice in a Collins glass. Float a ½ ounce of Aperol on top and garnish with a lemongrass stalk.

Lemongrass Syrup
6 stalks lemongrass, cut in 1-inch pieces
2 cups water
1 cup sugar

Steep lemongrass in water for 2 hours; transfer to blender and blend. Strain mixture and add sugar. Shake until blended.

. . . .

Stockholm Syndrome

Sarah Thomas, Spoon

1 ½ ounces Old Raj Blue Label Gin
1 ounce Pimms No. 1
1 ounce masala chai
½ ounce ginger syrup
2 dashes orange bitters

Combine ingredients in a mixing tin. Add ice and shake vigorously. Double strain into a chilled coupe. Garnish with a burnt orange peel.

. . . .

A Stranger in Town

Kiersten Schilinski, Dish Osteria

"This is a cocktail I had as a special at Dish for weeks—it is still one of my favorites. It was eventually put on the winter 2014 cocktail list at Maialino in New York City, though under a different moniker. I'll still make it as a special for some of my regulars in NYC. I love the addition of salt; it has the magical ability to brighten up the cocktail and bring out the vegetal qualities of Cynar. I would be curious to try this with the Cynar 70 proof for an even boozier alternative," says Schilinski.

1 ½ ounces Cynar
1 ounce Carpano Antica Formula
½ ounce Bulleit Bourbon
¼ ounce lemon juice
5 dashes orange bitters

Combine ingredients in a mixing tin. Add ice, shake and double strain into a chilled coupe glass. Garnish with a pinch of sea salt.

. . . .

Tiki Tea
Michelle Schubert, Tiki Lounge

1 ounce raspberry-infused vodka (recipe follows)
½ ounce Cherry Heering
½ ounce lime juice
½ ounce lemon juice
1 ounce demerara syrup
Fill: club soda

Shake and strain over fresh ice in a Collins glass and top with soda. Garnish with a lemon peel.

Raspberry-Infused Vodka
1 quart raspberries
2 750-milliliter bottles Stoichnaya Vodka

In a nonreactive container, lightly muddle raspberries to release juice. Add vodka. Let sit 2 to 3 days, tasting often to check desired flavor profile.

. . . .

Toit Annan
Lucas Felak

1 ½ ounces Chivas 12-Year Scotch Whisky
½ ounce Laphroaig 10-Year Scotch Whisky
1 ounce pineapple juice
½ ounce sage simple syrup
¼ ounce lemon juice

Combine ingredients in mixing tin, add ice and shake vigorously. Strain over crushed ice and Earl Grey tea leaves in a rocks glass. Add 2 dashes of rhubarb bitters.

. . . .

Triple Apple Kentucky Mule

Stephanie Dickson, Blue Dust

1 ½ ounces triple apple–infused bourbon (recipe follows)
2 dashes walnut bitters (recipe follows)
Fill: ginger beer

Build bourbon and bitters in copper mug over ice. Top with Natrona Bottling Co. Jamaican Ginger Hot! Hot! Hot! ginger beer and garnish with lemon twist.

Triple Apple–Infused Bourbon
12 apples (I like to use 4 Granny Smith apples for tartness, 4 Red Delicious apples for color and 4 either Pink Lady or Gala apples for sweetness and texture)
1 gallon bourbon
1 lemon

Core and slice apples into wedges. It is not necessary to peel the apples. Split the apples evenly among 2 1-gallon jars. Add ½ gallon of bourbon to each jar. Using a potato peeler, zest the lemon. Add half of the lemon zest to each jar. Cover jars and keep refrigerated for two weeks. The apples must be completely covered or they will spoil!

Walnut Bitters
½ teaspoon whole allspice
½ teaspoon black peppercorns
3 whole cinnamon sticks
½ cup walnuts, chopped
2 teaspoons grade A maple syrup
½ cup rye whiskey

Combine all ingredients in a 12-ounce mason jar. Store in the warmest part of your kitchen for two weeks. Shake mixture vigorously every other day.

. . . .

Turpentine Makes My Pussy Wet (or Power Bottom)
Erika "Jiggerfinger" Joyner

"This cocktail was named by Chef Justin Severino, Cure & Morcilla, Pittsburgh," noted Sean D. Enright.

1½ ounces Bourbon
½ ounce Benedictine
¼ ounce Combier Kümmel
2 dashes angostura bitters

Stir and pour over one large cube in a rocks glass. Garnish with an orange peel.

. . . .

uccello del paradiso
Lucky Munro and Will Groves

1 ounce Cynar 70
1 ounce Smith & Cross
¾ ounce Lime
¾ ounce Lucky's homemade orgeat (recipe follows)
7 dashes angostura bitters
2 pinches salt

Combine ingredients in mixing tin. Add ice and shake vigorously. Strain into short tin, dump ice and add 1 medium-sized ice cube. Shake until cube melts and double strain into a coupe glass. Garnish with 3 additional drops of angostura, à la whiskey sour.

Lucky's Homemade Orgeat
8 ounces unsweetened almond milk (containing xanthan gum, lecithin, or another emulsifier)
8 ounces turbinado sugar
8 drops orange blossom water
1 bar spoon organic almond extract

Place in an industrial-strength blender. Blend for 1½ minutes. Conversely, place mixture in a saucepan on the stove, heat and stir. Do not boil.

. . . .

The Van Buren

Frederick Arnold, Tender Bar + Kitchen

1½ ounces Wigle Genever
½ ounce green Chartreuse
½ ounce Benedictine
½ ounce dry vermouth
1 dash rhubarb bitters

Stir and strain on fresh ice in a rocks glass. Garnish with several drops of rose water.

. . . .

The Wes Suppressor

Jen Mulero, Shrubdown Shrub Cocktail Competition

1 sprig rosemary
¼ ounce green Chartreuse
2 ounces E&J Brandy
1 ounce plum rosemary shrub (recipe follows)
½ ounce honey syrup

Put 1 small sprig of rosemary on a plate and soak with green Chartreuse. Light on fire and snuff out with an overturned coupe glass. In a separate mixing tin, add remaining ingredients with ice. Shake and strain into the smoked-rosemary coupe. Garnish with a fresh rosemary sprig.

Plum Rosemary Shrub

1 quart plums sliced
1 quart local honey

5 sprigs rosemary
1 quart organic apple cider vinegar

Mix plums, local honey and rosemary and let sit overnight. Strain through a china hat, mashing as much liquid out as possible. Add organic apple cider vinegar. Store for 1 to 2 weeks, taste often. "Winner of Shrubdown Shrub Competition 2.0," says Mulero.

. . . .

Words Once Spoken
Rob Hirst

¾ ounce Meletti Amaro
¾ ounce apricot liqueur
¾ ounce lemon juice
½ ounce Luxardo Maraschino

Shake and double strain into a chilled cocktail coupe.

. . . .

Zihuatanejo
Chris Matrozza

1 ½ ounces strawberry-infused Milagro Blanco Tequila (recipe follows)
½ ounce Grand Marnier
¾ ounce lime juice
¾ ounce almond agave syrup (recipe follows)
1 egg white

Dry shake. Add ice, shake and strain into egg coupe.

Strawberry-Infused Milagro Blanco Tequila
Combine 1 quart fresh-sliced strawberries and 1 bottle tequila for 24 hours. Strain.

Almond Agave Syrup
1 cup almonds
1 cup agave nectar
1 cup water

Toast white almonds in oven until brown. Add almonds, agave nectar and water to blender and blend until smooth. Refrigerate.

13

THE EXOTIC TASTEMAKER

Photo by Adam Milliron.

Monique Ruvolo has an exotic flair to her dishes. She brings a Middle Eastern perspective combined with lessons she's taken from mentors and her mom. That background has created a unique dining experience to the tiki-themed Hidden Harbor.

"Those are my favorite dishes to this day—some of the ones my mom made," she said over the phone. "I try to make it more appealing to the masses. I try to expose people to what I've grown up with. My mom absolutely affected how I cook."

Ruvolo was born and raised in New Jersey. But her parents are from Cairo, Egypt. Her mother used a lot of traditional Egyptian recipes when she cooked for her family. And Ruvolo was also surrounded by a lot of different nationalities, which exposed her to different types of cuisines. The exposure to all those things made her a dynamic chef.

"The gorgonzola pairs nicely with beer," she said. "And the potato, they're deep fried. It really kind of highlighted our use of local beer. And if you're using them for cocktail, it pairs well with a sweet drink."

Caramelized Onion & Gorgonzola Croquette with Mustard Cream Sauce

Monique Ruvolo, Independent Brewing Company and Hidden Harbor

Makes 15 to 20

4 large russet potatoes
3 eggs
I cup caramelized onion (recipe follows)
I cup imported gorgonzola
I tablespoon ground cumin (toast first)
I tablespoon ground coriander (toast first)
I tablespoon red pepper flakes
3 tablespoons chives (chopped)
3 tablespoons parsley
I tablespoon salt-and-pepper blend
2 cups plain Italian bread crumbs
I cup plain panko bread crumbs

Rinse and then boil potatoes whole with skin until they are fork tender.
Peel skin and put through a ricer.
In a mixing bowl, add all the ingredients except bread crumbs and
    2 eggs.
Form small croquettes, typically a little smaller than a golf ball.
Dredge formed croquettes in eggs and then in bread crumbs.
Refrigerate for 30 minutes.
Deep fry until golden brown. Then serve with mustard sauce.

Caramelized Onion
2 medium white onions, diced
I tablespoon blended oil
3 tablespoons Arsenal cider or sweet white wine

Sauté onions in oil. Keep on a low heat until onions start to brown.
Finish with Arsenal cider or sweet white wine.

. . . .

Mustard Sauce

¼ cup brown mustard seeds
¼ cup yellow mustard seeds
1 cup amber/porter beer
¼ cup white vinegar
3 tablespoons sugar
1¼ cups heavy cream
1 tablespoon thyme
salt and pepper, to taste
1 cup Dijon mustard

Combine first five ingredients. Add heavy cream to mustard mixture and simmer until the liquid is reduced by half. Add thyme and salt and pepper to taste. Once the mixture is cool, add Dijon mustard. Serve sauce on the side.

14

PARTING WORDS FROM A PITTSBURGH BARTENDER

The evolution of Pittsburgh bartending has followed the evolution of the city. With each era, barkeeps in the city adapted to the times. Through the last 125 years, a tradition has been established by an array of immigrants, travelers and locals. In that tradition, there are basic rules to follow. They give an understanding of what a bartender must do every day.

Craft cocktailing dates back to the days of Kate Hester, when a bartender was central to the social and political trends of the day. Its local history continued through Prohibition with "Kid" Miller and was carried on by Joe Sala in the Great Depression and the 1940s. It is a trade that was celebrated in 1960s Shadyside and for decades thereafter. There is, and has always been, a place in Pittsburgh for a good bartender.

The rules are easy to grasp but are frequently missed by newcomers to the trade. A great bartender must know the "foundation" drinks intimately. Learning the first-generation cocktails, then studying their evolution into the modern classics we recognize today, gives a bartender the knowledge to create new cocktails. Too often up-and-coming bartenders attempt to design drinks that are simply unbalanced and lack any discernible flavor. Without understanding the basic principles of flavor and considering the cocktails that preceded today's, nothing new can hold up.

Study the history of each drink, recipe and spirit. Study absinthe regulation and the order of monks who distill Chartreuse. Study a city's bartending history and drinking culture; see how it touches nearly every facet of community, from nightlife to politics. An exceptional bartender does not merely craft a guest's drinks. They are also teachers.

Be prepared to fiercely debate the merits of using (or not using) Rose's Lime Juice in your gimlet, or who created the Tom & Jerry. What is the best method for shaking an egg in a cocktail? Does a Boulevardier get a lemon or an orange peel garnish?

It is important to understand the properties of every drink you make. Your judgment will come through tasting, note taking, industry events and personal preferences. Tasting is the most important aspect of learning these spirits. What is the difference between gin and Genever? Whiskey or whisky? After all, it will be your memories of the spirits that you will be explaining to the guests.

Always use fresh ingredients. No exceptions. No bottled orange juice, sours mixes, grenadine syrups, Rose's Lime Juice (except, maybe in that gimlet). My own personal preference is to fresh squeeze lime juice to order; presqueeze lemons daily. Oranges and grapefruits should be juiced every two to three days, depending on freshness determined by daily tasting. Sours mixes, grenadine, falernum and orgeat are all significantly better when the bartender prepared it. If you're using store-bought juices and mixers, then your cocktail could be made anywhere, by anyone. It isn't special or unique. For your guests, make it special and make it yours.

Knowing whether a cocktail should be stirred or shaken should eventually become intuitive to the accomplished bartender. The techniques themselves will, through continued practice, become easier to perfect. Nobody took a bar spoon and produced a perfect stir in his first foray behind the bar. With proper guidance and continued training you develop a style that becomes second nature. Stirring, shaking, straining, building, juicing, peeling, cutting and measuring—with practice, all of these techniques will have the fluidity and grace of a beautiful ballet to the customer.

Remember that bartenders work a lot like bakers. A baker follows a specific recipe with accurate measurements to acquire the proper result for breads and pastries. So, too, should a bartender follow predetermined recipes and measure exact amounts to ensure proper ratios for each cocktail.

The greatest joy you will achieve in this trade is when you have studied another person's instructions, and eventually after years of following your predecessors' guidelines, you create your own rules based on your experiences in the craft. This is how we all came to this agreement of knowledge, and it is how future generations in Pittsburgh will take craft cocktailing to the next level.

The fundamental idea behind this book is to share information with bartending compatriots. Pittsburgh has a close-knit community where sharing ideas and techniques are essential to growth. We discuss, debate and argue, but also—always—we listen. This sort of respectful camaraderie makes drinks, bars and cities better.

This is one bartender from Pittsburgh's chosen methods, culled from years of studying, training, education and practice. My methods often change when I am introduced to newer techniques that work better than my own. I only come to such conclusions by testing these ideas and applying them to my experiences behind the bar. This most recent cocktail revolution grew from forward-thinking bartenders breaking free of the boundaries of the previous established norms. Only by pushing the envelope and analyzing our predecessors' methods can we continue to evolve this craft. I look forward to learning from the next generation of bartenders.

—SEAN ENRIGHT

BIBLIOGRAPHY

All Pittsburgh Courier *articles were accessed via Pqarchiver.com. All* Pittsburgh Post-Gazette, Pittsburgh Daily Post *and* Pittsburgh Weekly Gazette *articles were accessed via Archives.post-gazette.com.*

Anderson, George. "The Tattler." *Pittsburgh Post-Gazette*, August 16, 1988, 13.
———. "Triangle Tattler: Encore Exits." *Pittsburgh Post-Gazette*, April 27, 1982, 48.
Barnes, Tom. "Business Growth Divides South Side." *Pittsburgh Post-Gazette*, September 19, 1989, 1.
———. "Protested South Side Bar Can Expand." *Pittsburgh Post-Gazette*, January 29, 1991, 7.
———. "Strip Is Jumping." *Pittsburgh Post-Gazette*, September 21, 1991, 4.
Batz, Bob, Jr. "Craft Beer Scene Hopping." *Pittsburgh Post-Gazette*, November 14, 1996, 36.
———. "Let's Go to the Hops." *Pittsburgh Post-Gazette*, May 30, 1997, 57.
———. "Nick's at Nite." *Pittsburgh Post-Gazette*, February 5, 1993, 54.
———. "Pews 'n' Brews." *Pittsburgh Post-Gazette*, August 1, 1996, 29.
Bernhard, Andrew. "Bartender No Longer Needs Long Repertory." *Pittsburgh Post-Gazette*, October 17, 1966, 2.
———. "On Higher Education." *Pittsburgh Post-Gazette*, September 3, 1976, 17.
Binder, Mary. "Closed Mic." *Pittsburgh City Paper*, March 22, 2000, 21–22, 24.
———. "Last Writes at Graffiti." *Pittsburgh City Paper*, March 22, 2000, 73–75.
———. "On Tap." *Pittsburgh City Paper*, September 12, 1996, 8–10.

Block, John R. "Mixologist! I'll Have a Moscow Mule." *Pittsburgh Post-Gazette*, August 24, 1976, 9.

Brennan, Lissa. "A Tale of Two Tappies." *In Pittsburgh*, April 15, 1998, 10–11.

Brooklyn Daily Eagle. "Fussfungle." January 19, 1902. Newspapers.com.

Browne, Joseph P. "Floating Night Club Proposed." *Pittsburgh Post-Gazette*, March 23, 1966, 25.

Clark, John L. "Deep Wylie." *Pittsburgh Courier*, March 30, 1929, 6.

———. "Pittsburgh." *Pittsburgh Courier*, June 12, 1926, 3.

———. "Wylie Avenue." *Pittsburgh Courier*, November 28, 1925, 3; January 18, 1930, 20; August 2, 1941, 14; October 4, 1941, 24; November 29, 1941, 14; April 20, 1946, 25; August 17, 1957, A1.

Cohen, Harold V. "The Drama Desk." *Pittsburgh Post-Gazette*, August 9, 1948, 18.

Coleman, Ted. "Waitresses Tell of 'Bar Room Romeos—'Trust-Bugs'; Fickle, Disagreeable Customers Make Job Difficult." *Pittsburgh Courier*, March 15, 1941, 3.

Connelly, Brian. "The New South Side." *Pittsburgh Newsweekly*, July 13, 1995, 6–8.

Cope, Myron. "Pittsburgh's Exotic Cocktail Lounges." *Pittsburgh Post-Gazette*, November 20, 1960, 6.

Coulson, Crocker. "Never Too Young for Nightclub Fun." *Pittsburgh Post-Gazette*, July 13, 1985, 4.

Crawford, Jane. "What They're Wearing at Metropol." *Pittsburgh Post-Gazette*, August 16, 1988, 11.

Danver, Charles. "Pittsburghesque." *Pittsburgh Post-Gazette*, January 22, 1926, 20; January 3, 1928, 6; January 14, 1928, 6; July 10, 1928, 8; November 27, 1928, 8; February 28, 1929, 10; March 27, 1930, 8; July 16, 1930, 6; September 19, 1930, 10; December 2, 1930, 8; January 9, 1931, 8; July 23, 1931, 6; July 28, 1931, 6; October 20, 1931, 8; November 28, 1931, 8; May 30, 1932, 10; June 14, 1932, 8; July 15, 1932, 8; October 25, 1932, 8; November 10, 1932, 8; December 9, 1932, 10; January 31, 1933, 8; May 10, 1933, 6; March 8, 1934; March 14, 1934, 10; June 11, 1934, 6; June 5, 1935, 10; June 17, 1935, 6; July 30, 1936; December 7, 1936, 8; January 15, 1937, 10; December 17, 1937, 8; August 22, 1938, 6; May 24, 1940, 13; September 9, 1940, 8; January 3, 1942, 6; January 15, 1942, 8; February 28, 1942, 6; March 11, 1942; April 27, 1944, 21, 8; April 14, 1945, 6; June 22, 1951, 27; December 15, 1956, 19; November 25, 1958, 35; January 3, 1959, 33; January 6, 1958, 29; February 6, 1959, 27; March 23, 1959, 31; June 15, 1959, 31; June 24, 1959, 31; July 17,

1960, 17; January 29, 1960, 25; August 5, 1960, 33; December 11, 1960, 26; June 23, 1961, 29; November 3, 1961, 33; September 24, 1962, 41.

Day, Jimmy. "'A Good Thing' Came to Clarence Mays—He Waited." *Pittsburgh Courier*, August 25, 1965, 23.

DeSena, Mary. "Like a Hurricane." *Pittsburgh Post-Gazette*, October 6, 1995, 79.

Fitzpatrick, Dan. "Latin Club to Open Downtown." *Pittsburgh Post-Gazette*, December 27, 2001, 21.

Fuoco, Michael. "How the South Side Got Its Groove Back." *Pittsburgh Post-Gazette*, July 7, 2002, 53.

———. "Strip a Funky, Happening Place." *Pittsburgh Post-Gazette*, August 6, 2000, 21.

Galle, Deborah. "Lift a Stein, Bend an Elbow or Two at Penn Brewery." *Pittsburgh Post-Gazette*, June 26, 1994, 118.

Green Goods Man. "A New Tipple on the South Side." *Pittsburgh Daily Post*, October 15, 1902, 10.

———. "Not a Success." *Pittsburgh Daily Post*, October 11, 1916, 11.

———. "Rabbit Cotton Farm." *Pittsburgh Daily Post*, September 13, 1913, 11.

———. "Whisky Rickey Crop Assured." *Pittsburgh Daily Post*, May 31, 1901, 9.

Guidry, Nate. "1940 to 1959: The Jazz Age in Pittsburgh." *Pittsburgh Post-Gazette*, April 18, 2004, G11.

———. "Stairway to Music." *Pittsburgh Post-Gazette*, July 1, 2007, 45.

Guo, David. "Disco Madness Seizes City, More on Way." *Pittsburgh Post-Gazette*, August 16, 1976, 15.

———. "Two Bars Busily Quenching Thirsts in Mt. Lebanon." *Pittsburgh Post-Gazette*, March 14, 1977, 11.

Harper, Colter. "'The Crossroads of the World': A Social and Cultural History of Jazz in Pittsburgh's Hill District, 1920–1970." Diss., Duquesne University, 2001.

Hayes, John. "Hot Spots." *Pittsburgh Post-Gazette*, March 15, 2003, 76.

———. "Loss of Metropol Is a Blow to Concerts in 1,000-Seat Range." *Pittsburgh Post-Gazette*, October 18, 2003, 36.

———. "Rosebud to Close After This Weekend." *Pittsburgh Post-Gazette*, January 30, 2004, 64.

Hayes, John, and Rouvalis, Cristina. "Wild Things." *Pittsburgh Post-Gazette*, December 11, 1998, 110.

Holland, Bernard. "Birdie Says Bye Bye to Hurricane, All That Jazz." *Pittsburgh Post-Gazette*, February 4, 1980, 1.

Hoover, Bob. "Mad Mex Brings New Beers to City." *Pittsburgh Post-Gazette*, December 30, 1993, 24.

———. "The Place to Be: 1900–1919: Music Halls and Amusement Parks." *Pittsburgh Post-Gazette*, April 18, 2004, G1.

Hopper, Justin. "Staging Rally." *Pittsburgh City Paper*, March 22, 2000, 23.

Hritz, Thomas M. "47 Years Behind Bar, It's Storytelling Time as Mixologist Retires." *Pittsburgh Post-Gazette*, March 5, 1979, 2.

Jannuzi, Gene. "'Auld Lang Syne' Sung as Nixon Closes for Good." *Pittsburgh Post-Gazette*, May 1, 1950, 1.

Johnson, Vince. "Epicure's New Cocktail Honors Princess Grace." *Pittsburgh Post-Gazette*, January 25, 1956, 15.

———. "'Puddler' Stumps Expert." *Pittsburgh Post-Gazette*, May 21, 1954, 19.

Jones, Diana Nelson, and John Hayes. "Bars in the 'Hood." *Pittsburgh Post-Gazette*, January 24, 1992, 32.

Kalina, Mike. "Area Discos Hopping as Business Thrives." *Pittsburgh Post-Gazette*, February 6, 1978, 1.

———. "Country Music Fans Buck Disco Trend in Own Club." *Pittsburgh Post-Gazette*, January 23, 1981, 25.

———. "Dining Out." *Pittsburgh Post-Gazette*, May 4, 1984, 28.

———. "His Big Dream." *Pittsburgh Post-Gazette*, August 22, 1989, 17.

———. "It's Disco Fever on Sunday Night." *Pittsburgh Post-Gazette*, January 31, 1979, 26.

———. "Mirage Is More Than Illusion on Nightclub Scene." *Pittsburgh Post-Gazette*, July 27, 1984, 17.

———. "Music Makers." *Pittsburgh Post-Gazette*, February 7, 1977, 13.

———. "Punk Goes the Trend." *Pittsburgh Post-Gazette*, January 30, 1981, 19.

Leonard, Vince. "Metropol: Industrial Dancing in the Strip." *Pittsburgh Post-Gazette*, August 12, 1988, 20.

Lord, Rich. "Culture Clash." *Pittsburgh City Paper*, December 18, 1996, 16–18.

Machamar, Peter. "Local Barkeeps Give Cocktails Irish Twist." *Pittsburgh Post-Gazette*, March 13, 1985, 28.

Masley, Ed. "Bands on the Run." *Pittsburgh Post-Gazette*, January 7, 2004, 33.

———. "1980 to Present: The Age of Rock." *Pittsburgh Post-Gazette*, April 18, 2004, G12.

McCart, Melissa. "Destination Dining." *Pittsburgh Post-Gazette*, October 17, 2013, 74.

———. "Hopped Up." *Pittsburgh Post-Gazette*, June 6, 2013, 56.

———. "Is There a Cook Shortage?" *Pittsburgh Post-Gazette*, August 18, 2013, 41.

———. "Still Coming of Age." *Pittsburgh Post-Gazette*, December 26, 2013, 70.

McDonald, Deborah. "Cuban Cool." *Pittsburgh Newsweekly*, August 6, 1997, 28.

McGough, Mike. "Walnut Street Is No Longer Mecca for the Young People." *Pittsburgh Post-Gazette*, January 1, 1972, 13.

Merriman, Woodene. "Church Brew Works Unveils New Menu, Wine List." *Pittsburgh Post-Gazette*, February 13, 1997, 63.

———. "Mad Mex Branching Across Town." *Pittsburgh Post-Gazette*, September 11, 1994, 105.

———. "Mexican Invasion." *Pittsburgh Post-Gazette*, December 17, 1993, 73.

———. "Take a Spin Through the New Vertigo Bar." *Pittsburgh Post-Gazette*, October 20, 1996, 94.

Mervis, Scott. "Cocktail Hour." *Pittsburgh Post-Gazette*, November 8, 1996, 71.

———. "Groovy Times." *Pittsburgh Post-Gazette*, August 11, 1995, 48.

———. "1960 to 1979: A Revolutionary Era." *Pittsburgh Post-Gazette*, April 18, 2004, G11.

———. "Rock in a Hard Place." *Pittsburgh Post-Gazette*, October 13, 2005, 100.

Millman, China. "Big Things from Big Burrito." *Pittsburgh Post-Gazette*, August 25, 2011, 64.

———. "A Drink Among Friends." *Pittsburgh Post-Gazette*, April 19, 2012, 71.

———. "In a Sea of Casual Cocktails, High-End Drinks Are Just Getting Better." *Pittsburgh Post-Gazette*, April 10, 2008, W19.

———. "Salt of the Earth Raises the Bar on Cocktails." *Pittsburgh Post-Gazette*, November 11, 2010, 73.

———. "Squeezed Out?" *Pittsburgh Post-Gazette*, October 20, 2011, 64.

Morris, Ken. "The Night." *New Pittsburgh Courier*, February 13, 1971, 12; February 20, 1971, 14; February 27, 1971, 12; August 7, 1971, 14.

———. "The Night Owl's…Pub Prowl." *Pittsburgh Courier*, August 25, 1973, 18.

———. "The Night Owl's Pub Prowl." *Pittsburgh Courier*, June 14, 1975, 19.

New York Times. "The Illegal Speak-Easies." July 6, 1891, 2.

Norman, Tony. "The Cocktail Twins." *Pittsburgh Post-Gazette*, November 22, 1996, 66.

———. "Era Comes to an End at Crawford Grill." *Pittsburgh Post-Gazette*, December 18, 1997, 57.

Olup, Carole. "On the Rocks." *Pittsburgh Post-Gazette*, November 26, 1986, 344.

Paris, Barry. "Suds Supplies Dwindling in Walkout at Iron City." *Pittsburgh Post-Gazette*, May 2, 1981, 8.

Pittsburgh Courier. "African Art a Boon to New 'Watusi' Drink." April 7, 1973, 28.
———. "Article 1—No title." September 26, 1959, A1.
———. "Big Time at Cotton Club Thursday." December 8, 1934, 9.
———. "Classified Ad 2." August 12, 1939, 20.
———. "The Cotton Club Is Here to Stay." August 25, 1934, 9.
———. "Display Ad 72." July 8, 1939, 20.
———. "Final Rites Held for James Banks." April 20, 1946, 3.
———. "Fullerton Café to Present Jack Spruce and Band." September 16, 1939, 9.
———. "Goings On About Town." June 30, 1962, 24.
———. "The Griddle." April 25, 1925, 9.
———. "Gus Greenlee's Crawford Grill to Open Formally Next Tuesday." January 6, 1934, 6.
———. "Javo's Jungle Is Classiest Night Club in the City." October 5, 1935, 17. Newspapers.com.
———. "Merdis Thomas. Bobby Jones, 3, Phil Carter Stay at Flamingo." February 19, 1955, 20.
———. "Mixologist." April 22, 1939, 21.
———. "New Mgrs. at Local Clubs." March 12, 1977, 18.
———. "Photo Standalone 50—No Title." May 19, 1945, 20.
———. "Photo Standalone 19—No Title." February 26, 1955, 19.
———. "Photo Standalone 27." March 30, 1957: A19.
———. "Popular Bartender Buried." January 28, 1956, 17.
———. "Popular Mixologist." June 28, 1941, 20.
———. "Rev. Hightower Stirs City Officials with Vice Disclosures." May 5, 1928, 9.
———. "Sam Haney Is an Expert Mixologist." January 11, 1941, 21.
———. "Tom West Murdered in Grill." July 27, 1946, 1.
Pittsburgh Daily Post. "Braddock Highball Beats Cook Cocktail." September 8, 1909, 9.
———. "The City Can Put It Down." March 7, 1890, 2.
———. "City Police Will Help Dry Agent Enforce Prohibition." May 22, 1921.
———. "The Club Room Speak-Easy." March 10, 1890, 2.
———. "Delmont Cafe Owner Named." May 11, 1927, 1.
———. "Denounced Speakeasies." January 13, 1902, 2.
———. "Depths of Degradation." October 28, 1889, 2.
———. "An Entirely New Method." October 27, 1890, 2.
———. "Exclusively to Families." March 8, 1890, 2.

————. "Had Lots of Liquor on Tap." May 16, 1892, 2.

————. "In the Wet South Side." February 7, 1890, 1.

————. "Lee Frazier Is Arrested." January 10, 1894.

————. "Local Affairs." August 4, 1870, 1.

————. "More Flogging." March 14, 1892, 1.

————. "Poisoned as Animals." October 2, 1923.

————. "A Portable Speakeasy." September 13, 1893, 3.

————. "Prohibition Squads Ready to 'Dry Up' Pittsburgh." March 9, 1923, 1.

————. "Reign of the Speak-Easy." March 5, 1890, 2.

————. "Rough on Speakeasies." September 2, 1889, 2.

————. "Rough on the Speakeasies." January 6, 1890, 2.

————. "A 'Society' Speakeasy." June 26, 1893, 4.

————. "Speakeasies Must Close." May 12, 1890, 2.

————. "Speakeasies on Tap." June 15, 1891, 4.

————. "Speak-Easy Owners Seen." February 4, 1890, 3.

————. "A Tale of Two Cities." September 22, 1890, 2.

————. "Those Club Speakeasies." October 10, 1892, 4.

————. "Traffic in Licenses." June 25, 1895, 5.

————. "Unlawful Liquor." August 26, 1893, 1.

————. "Waiting for the List." April 10, 1891, 8.

Pittsburgh Post-Gazette. "The Bartender as Psychiatrist." March 8, 1972, 12.

————. "Bartenders Get Day's Receipts When Old North Side Tavern Closes, Due to Prohibition." October 28, 1919, 9.

————. "Best Dining: Unexpected Trends." December 18, 2014, 105.

————. "Blakely Makes War on the Speakeasy." March 5, 1912, 1.

————. "Bootleg Clan Here Glum as Repeal Near." November 9, 1933, 15.

————. "City Scenes: Down by the Riverside." June 29, 1991, 9.

————. "Closing Hour Throws 'Speaks' into Turmoil." March 23, 1933, 32.

————. "Dry Law Repeal Brings No Sign of Spree Here." December 7, 1933, 1.

————. "Final Curtain Will Drop Tonight at the Nixon." April 29, 1950, 1.

————. "Flames Peril New Boatel." May 15, 1964, 1.

————. "Gives Clark Moonshine, Map of Where to Buy It." September 8, 1928, 13.

————. "A Grand Old Party for Grand Old Party." October 27, 1967, 21.

————. "Hill No Longer Mecca of Jazz Greats." March 25, 1975, 1.

————. "Liquor Ring Leaders Say Exposure Has Been Halted." November 28, 1922, 2.

———. "Lot of Trouble at Club." March 26, 1961, 3.

———. "Manhattan Cocktail Most Popular with Local Folk." December 28, 1934, 10.

———. "Mario Takes Turn as Critic." June 5, 1993, 30.

———. "Metropol Previews What's New." August 19, 1988, 38.

———. "Old Man 1929 Is Buried Under Assorted Bottles." January 1, 1930, 1.

———. "Police Captain Makes Record by Conducting One-Man Raid." January 27, 1908, 2.

———. "Rees Design-Sales Provides Talent for City's Rock 'n' Roll Hall of Stars." April 21, 1992, 17.

Pittsburgh Weekly Gazette. "All Kinds of Drinks Are Easy to Obtain in Either City on the Sabbath." December 22, 1901, 1.

———. "Honey O'Neil's Diamond Street Speakeasy Was Also Visited." December 17, 1902, 2.

———. "Police Adopt Vile, Shallow Plan to Make Speakeasies Possible." December 21, 1902, 2.

———. "Priest Raids Speakeasy and Scatters the Inmates." November 25, 1901, 1.

———. "Sunday Scenes of Disorder among Allegheny Speakeasies." November 11, 1901, 1.

———. "Too Much Talking Riled M'Aleese." July 28, 1902, 2.

———. "Value of Homes Has Come Down." November 12, 1901, 1.

Pitz, Marylynne. "1920 to 1939: From Speakeasies to Harlem Nights." *Pittsburgh Post-Gazette*, April 18, 2004: G10.

———. "Pegasus Springing Forth." *Pittsburgh Post-Gazette*, December 7, 2009, 17.

Potocki, Chris. "Out of Their Skulls." *Pittsburgh Newsweekly.* March 13, 1997, 22.

Pulizzi, David. "The Age of Decade-nce." *Pittsburgh City Paper*, October 21, 1998, 34.

Rouvalis, Cristina. "It's Beer Darwinism." *Pittsburgh Post-Gazette*, May 2, 1997, 31.

Sheehan, Andrew. "'Heaven' to Be Reincarnated as 'Mirage.'" *Pittsburgh Post-Gazette*, May 23, 1984, 4.

———. "Ticked Off." *Pittsburgh Post-Gazette*, January 31, 1987, 4.

Taylor, John G. "Bartender's Union Draws Color Line." *Pittsburgh Courier*, September 20, 1941, 21.

Toland, Bill. "Are You a Bartender Named Lily? Get Guild-ed." *Pittsburgh Post-Gazette*, March 17, 2011, 42.

———. "Bottle Slinger Is Shaking Up Cocktail Scene." *Pittsburgh Post-Gazette*, December 9, 2009, 31.

———. "Cobbler: A Half-Baked Cocktail." *Pittsburgh Post-Gazette*, April 1, 2012, 69.

———. "First-Ever Cocktail Week Set." *Pittsburgh Post-Gazette*, September 8, 2013, 73.

———. "Tender Is the Night Spot." *Pittsburgh Post-Gazette*, February 28, 2013, 27.

———. "Whiskey 101: A Food-Studies Course." *Pittsburgh Post-Gazette*, August 1, 2013, 29.

Toland, Bill, and China Millman. "Whiskey Rebels." *Pittsburgh Post-Gazette*, February 2, 2012, 40.

Washington, Chester L. "Deep Wylie." *Pittsburgh Courier*, February 9, 1929, 7.

———. "Pittsburgh's Harlem." *Pittsburgh Courier*, September 3, 1927, 7.

———. "Repeal Hits the 'Avenooe'!" *Pittsburgh Courier*, December 9, 1933, 6.

———. "Up and Down the Avenue." *Pittsburgh Courier*, December 31, 1938, 16; February 18, 1939, 9; April 8, 1939, 11; March 11, 1939, 9; March 25, 1939, 9; May 13, 1939, 11.

Whelan, Sean. "Beer Witness." *Pittsburgh City Paper*, October 7, 1998, 26–27.

Yates, Edward. "Start One of Their Own." *Pittsburgh Post-Gazette*, January 8, 1962, 17.

ABOUT THE AUTHORS

Cody McDevitt is an award-winning journalist who works full time for the *Somerset Daily American*. His work has appeared in the *Pittsburgh Post-Gazette*, *Table* magazine and *Pittsburgh Quarterly*. Local media praised him for his exposé on casinos in western Pennsylvania that appeared in *Belt* magazine's Pittsburgh Anthology. His dream is to one day own a home at Hidden Valley or Seven Springs so he can wake up and ski before going to work.

Sean Enright is one of the founding fathers of the craft cocktail movement in Pittsburgh. He has managed many of Pittsburgh's most prestigious restaurants and helped found the Pittsburgh Chapter of the United States Bartenders' Guild. Sean has also been active in the Pittsburgh art community, where he produced a literary art magazine called *yawp*. Sean is currently working on opening his first bar in Pittsburgh. He continues to consult and mentor the next generation of service industry professionals.